ARCHETICTURE

ARCHETICTURE

Ecstasies of Space, Time, and the Human Body

David Farrell Krell

State University of New York Press

Cover photo: Marq Bailey, 1995
Cover Art:
Donald L. Bates and Peter Davidson
LAB Architectural Studios, London.
Bates and Davison are the winners of the 1997 "Federation Square"
competition in Melbourne. Pictured on the cover is a detail of
their design for Wagga Wagga, Australia, 1995.

Published by

State University of New York Press

© 1997 David Farrell Krell

*For information, address State University of New York Press
State University Plaza, Albany, NY 12246*

*Production by Dana Foote
Marketing by Nancy Farrell*

Library of Congress Cataloging-in-Publication Data

Krell, David Farrell.
Archeticture : ecstasies of space, time, and the human body /
David Farrell Krell.
p.   cm.
Includes bibliographical references and index.
ISBN 0–7914–3409–5 (hc : alk. paper). — ISBN 0–7914–3410–9 (pbk.
: alk. paper)
1. Architecture—Philosophy. I. Title.
NA2500.K72 1997
720' .1--dc2
97–30057
CIP

10 9 8 7 6 5 4 3 2 1

for
Don Bates

CONTENTS

ILLUSTRATIONS

ABBREVIATIONS

BW   Martin Heidegger, *Basic Writings,* ed. D. F. Krell, 2d rev. ed.
(San Francisco: HarperCollins, 1993).

DAF   Rudolf Arnheim, *The Dynamics of Architectural Form*
(Berkeley: University of California Press, 1977).

E   Luce Irigaray, *Éthique de la différence sexuelle* (Paris: Minuit,
1984).

EpW   G. W. F. Hegel, *Enzyklopädie der philosophischen Wissenschaften im Grundriß, zweiter Teil, Die Naturphilosophie,* in
Werke in zwanzig Bänden, Theorie Werkausgabe (Frankfurt
am Main: Suhrkamp, 1970).

GP   Martin Heidegger, *Die Grundprobleme der Phänomen-
ologie,* vol. 24 of *Martin Heidegger Gesamtausgabe* (Frankfurt am Main: V. Klostermann, 1975).

I   Jacques Derrida, Introduction to *L'Origine de la géométrie,*
by Edmund Husserl, trans. Jacques Derrida (Paris: Presses
Universitaires de France, 1962).

K   Jacques Derrida, *Khôra* (Paris: Galilée, 1993).

KPM   Martin Heidegger, *Kant und das Problem der Metaphysik,*
4th exp. ed. (Frankfurt am Main: V. Klostermann, 1973).

KrV-A   Immanuel Kant, *Kritik der reinen Vernunft,* 1st ed. (1781;
reprint, Hamburg: F. Meiner, 1956).

KrV-B   Immanuel Kant, *Kritik der reinen Vernunft,* 2d ed. (1787;
reprint, Hamburg: F. Meiner, 1956).

KSA   Friedrich Nietzsche, *Kritische Studienausgabe,* ed. Giorgio
Colli and Mazzino Montinari, 15 vols. (Berlin and Munich:
W. de Gruyter and DTV, 1980).

MA   Martin Heidegger, *Metaphysische Anfangsgründe der Logik
im Ausgang von Leibniz,* vol. 26 of *Martin Heidegger
Gesamtausgabe* (Frankfurt am Main: V. Klostermann, 1978).

P   Maurice Merleau-Ponty, *Phénoménologie de la perception* (Paris: Gallimard, 1945).

PGZ   Martin Heidegger, *Prolegomena zur Geschichte des Zeitbegriffs,* vol. 20 of *Martin Heidegger Gesamtausgabe* (Frankfurt am Main: V. Klostermann, 1979).

S   E. T. A. Hoffmann, *Der Sandmann* (Stuttgart: P. Reclam, 1991).

StA   Sigmund Freud, *Studienausgabe,* ed. Alexander Mitscherlich et al., 12 vols. (Frankfurt am Main: S. Fischer, 1982).

SZ   Martin Heidegger, *Sein und Zeit,* 12th ed. (Tübingen: M. Niemeyer, 1972).

UG   Edmund Husserl, "Der Ursprung der Geometrie," in *Die Krisis der europäischen Wissenschaften und die transzendentale Phänomenologie,* ed. Walter Biemel, vol. 6 of *Husserliana* (The Hague: Martinus Nijhoff, 1954).

V   Maurice Merleau-Ponty, *Le visible et l'invisible* (Paris: Gallimard, 1964).

VA   G. W. F. Hegel, *Vorlesungen über die Ästhetik II,* in *Werke in zwanzig Bänden,* Theorie Werkausgabe (Frankfurt am Main: Suhrkamp, 1970).

VE   Georges Bataille, *Visions of Excess: Selected Writings, 1927–1939,* ed. Allan Stoekl (Manchester, U.K.: Manchester University Press, 1985).

PREFACE

For whom has this book been written? For that group of architects who have the unshakable habit of theory, and for those philosophers who, one way or another, have been shaken into an awareness of architecture. Perhaps these two groups are growing, as architects accept the fact that they are not engineers, and do not even want to be engineers, and philosophers struggle with the realization that they are not alone in the world of theory.

No doubt, this book falls between two stools—the stool of the designer at the drawing table, and that of the philosopher, which looks something like the Delphic tripod. I cannot claim competence in architecture or the history of architecture; my competence in philosophy and the history of philosophy is equally uneven. I have therefore tried to make this a very small book, and have tried to remember to be modest in the presentation of my thesis.

I am grateful to the following persons and institutions for permission to use the illustrations that appear in the present volume: for the prints by William Blake, to Marilyn Hunt and the Yale Center for British Art; for the prints by Leonardo da Vinci, to the publishers of *Leonardo on the Human Body,* trans. Charles D. O'Malley and J. B. de C. M. Saunders (New York: Dover Publications, 1983); and for the prints by Piranesi, to Sarah J. Sibbald and the National Gallery of Art. My particular gratitude to John Hejduk and Rizzoli International for permission to reprint his haunting *Passage* from *Vladivostok* (New York: Rizzoli International, 1989), and to Gisela

Baurmann for the series of original works gathered under the title "Quetsch: Investigation into Architectural Representation."

Chapter 1 is a revised version of a lecture presented at the Graduate School of Design, Harvard University, on October 8, 1991; my thanks to Mohsen Mostáfavi. Earlier forms of chapter 2 were presented as papers to the Architectural Association, London, in November 1987, to the Summer Studio in Architecture, directed by Daniel Libeskind at the Villa Olmo in Como, in July 1988, and to the School of Architecture, University of Florida, Gainesville, in November 1989. My thanks to Don Bates and Peter Davidson, Ben Nicholson, Jeff Kipnis, and Daniel Libeskind for their help and support. The archetictural sections of Heidegger and Freud in chapter 3—dedicated to Gisela Baurmann, who provided the graphics for it—took their departure from an event sponsored by DePaul University's College of Liberal Arts and Sciences and The Graham Foundation: the conference, *"Das Unheimliche:* Philosophy • Architecture • The City," which took place on 26-27 April 1991 at DePaul. My thanks to all the participants, among them Jacques Derrida, Daniel Libeskind, Don Bates, Stanley Tigerman, Ben Nicholson, Jeff Kipnis, Mark Rakatansky, Catherine Ingraham, and Peter Eisenman. An early version of chapter 4 appeared in *Philosophy Today,* 35, no. 1 (Spring 1991): 43-50, dedicated to Robert Lechner; my thanks to the editor of *Philosophy Today,* David Pellauer. Finally, the appendix was first presented as a seminar at the Berlin Architecture Workshop in summer 1996. My thanks to Don Bates, Peter Davidson, and Gisela Baurmann.

Many of the texts inserted into my own text are from two works that have inspired me in a special way: my thanks for the continuing work of Luce Irigaray and Jacques Derrida. For the inserts, I have relied most heavily on Luce Irigaray, *Éthique de la différence sexuelle* (Paris: Minuit, 1984), and Jacques Derrida, *Khôra* (Paris: Galilée, 1993). At the time my own book was written, no English translations of these books were available, and so I provided my own translations. I cite these two works at the end of my inserts as either *E* or *K,* with page number. The inserts from John Hejduk's "The Albatross Screeched" appear in Daniel Libeskind, *Countersign* (London: Academy Editions, 1991), 122.

Special thanks to Peter Davidson of LAB Architectural Studios, London, who has been a loyal friend to this book and to me; also to David Thomas, who assisted me at every stage of the project. Over the years, and at various times and in sundry ways, Gisela Baurmann, John Hejduk, Daniel Libeskind, Sabine Mödersheim, Ben Nicholson, and Stanley Tigerman have befriended the project and inspired me. Its guiding genius has always been Don Bates.

Chicago   D. F. K.

INTRODUCTION
Archeticture—Spell It New?

> *O architecture! A mere reflection in the waters of remembrance?*
> *The memories of your future in the company of my cherished*
> *Polya abound!*
> —Alberto Pérez-Gómez

> They [that is, the Russian constructivists] were saying "make a
> new order," but, more important, they were saying
> "make it with your body."
> —Robert J. Yudell

W e are at the end of the troubled century in which Ezra
Pound encouraged poets to "make it new." At the end
of such a century, one that brings to its end a jaundiced
millennium, it is doubtless quaint to call for renovation, if only in
orthography. Why make it new? The forces of reaction and accommodation have shown us that there is always a paved road that will
conduct us back to a tried-and-true tradition. Reaction too is
smooth, even slick: it may well lead into its end a century and a
saeculum that will be remembered (but by whom?) primarily for its
slickness. A few fires burning out of control along the way, to be
sure; numberless deaths during these final hundred years; but for

1

the most part, in architecture as in all things, packaging and lubrication—slickness.

I begin with these jaded remarks on the new conservatism
because I want to conjure what I can least accept; conjure it by
means of an apotropaic ritual, a voodoo operation that puts a few
pins in, acupuncture for military purposes. The slick way back—or
ahead, for that matter—has always been and will always be available. The irony is that no architect or student of architecture ought
to be fooled by packaging or mollified by lubrication, even as they
are being asked to produce increasing amounts of it along the
career path of infinite accommodation. Is self-deception easier or
more difficult in architecture today, where the temptations to capitulation and conformity are omnipresent and the road to them
always smoothed? No obstacles. Or so it seems.

For it may well be that architecture (still spelling it old, for the
moment) is now in full crisis. The century began with crises in all
the sciences, in mathematics, and the arts; crises of capitalism, crises
of representative government, crises of social order, crises of human
identity. Perhaps there has been no time for crisis in architecture
until now: a century and a millennium of fire and destruction is a
busy time for planners, designers, and builders. Perhaps only now
can architects in Europe, America, and Japan reap the dubious fruits
of protracted unemployment and lingering underemployment.
Perhaps only now will architecture find the time to ask what it is up
to and how low it can go.

As the world speeds up, producing weapons that get smarter
and smarter and politicians who grow more and more obtuse, an
uncanny slowdown seems to be occurring. Not on all sides, to be
sure, but in the occasional nook and cranny one sees the architectural studio becoming a place of *learning*—of learning *about* learn-

ing, of learning *from* architecture what the possibilities *of* architecture may be. As hectic as a student's life has to be in the studio, trying to assert her or his ego, gift, ambition, or dream against the crushing sarcasms that pour from the mouths of egos and ambitions that have all the advantages of experience and power, there are now suddenly moments of uncanny respite and calm. Even though the tried-and-true tradition of architectural education still flourishes (the pedagogy of humiliation and exhaustion, of perpetual prodding and poking, with sideways slaps at the master's competitors); and even though the survival strategies of youth persist (trying to work against time and all the odds in order to assert one's space in an overcrowded room); even though, in a word, life in the studio remains relentlessly harried and harrowing, there are moments of interruption. Earlier in the century we would have called them epiphanies—manifestations of *quidditas* in *claritas,* of essence in radiance. Now they are temporary work stoppages, intermittent truncations, momentary voids or lulls. During these moments of depletion and dislocation—of *désœuvrement*—both master and apprentice, joined now by the chastened philosopher, observe the languid procession of things they have never understood very well, things they still cannot manipulate or control, passing by in review. Let me mention a few of them.

   1. We do not know what *space* is. We know only that space and place alike recede from our geometries, frustrating the measuring rods and calipers we once spread so confidently across Gaia, the Earth.

   2. We do not know what *time* is. We know only that our calendars and clocks have their own history, their own eras, and that their rule is therefore never to be trusted. We know that in modernity time's time finally came, culminating in Nietzsche's thought of

the eternal recurrence of the same, Bergson's *durée*, Freud's dream-like immortality of the unconscious, Husserl's internal time-consciousness, and Heidegger's analysis of human existence as ecstatic temporality—too many convincing answers to too many vague questions about time.

3. We do not know what the *human body* is. We know only that we are obliged to house it and provide public spaces for it. According to an ancient tradition, the body is the house of the soul—if only in the form of the modern muddled psyche. The body is viewed variously as a machine, a prison cell, a glory, or a plague, a beauty or a beast that continues to elude architecture.

4. We do not know what *cities* are, especially our own, or whether and under what circumstances they might be viable, habitable, livable.

5. We do not know how close we are to the destruction without possible recovery of the little corner of the universe that we call *nature*.

Finally, to end the list, we do not know whether in our day-to-day exertions in our studies or studios we are equipping ourselves to deal with these immense problems or merely submitting to the processes that level, flatten, and anesthetize everyone who participates in them. We do not know if we are merely teasing ourselves with our little clevernesses, learning to be satisfied with divertissement, happy enough with distractions, if that is all there is, until the weasel goes pop.

What I write here and now—and have written throughout this modest text of four chapters—may be only a distraction. That is to say, it may well *fail* to distract architects from their work. I do have to try to distract them, of course, if only out of ressentiment. For when architects are at work they are incomprehensible to the philosopher: they are the high priests and priestesses of the design studio—in a universe made by design, where only architects can be at home and the philosopher is outside, shivering, nose pressed against the windowpane.

Space, time, the human body, the city, the environment, and the universe of design. As the Joker says to Bob, "There's so much to do, and so little time." Let me therefore start with the universe— the universe of space, time, and the human body.

Timaeus of Locri, the main speaker of Plato's *Timaeus* and of my own first chapter, covered the theme of the universe in a day, and I shall be even more concise. If Timaeus's discourse is merely "probable" or "likely," as he himself says, I shall have to settle for sheer improbability and unseemly haste. Yet I *must* start with the universe—for it was planned and constructed in a cosmic design studio by the Demiurge.

Demi-urge: it sounds like half-an-inclination, a minor tickle, or a demi-semi-quaver under the belt. But no. Δῆμος is the community, especially of the "common people"; ἐργάνη is the worker, especially the skilled artisan or craftsman. His is not an "urge" but an "erg," an exertion guided by skill or know-how, τέχνη. The Demiurge designs and builds the universe with *technique.* However, whether we think of him as artisan or proletarian, the People's Worker or the skilled laborer, this cosmic technician is called by another name in the discourse of Timaeus, a more disconcerting and even embarrassing name: he is called the maker *and father* of the universe (*Timaeus* 28c 3). *Father* of the universe? What can that mean? What is the relation between architectonics and paternity?

Chapter 1 recalls the oldest philosophical story about the making of the universe. Plato's Timaeus, a Pythagorean astronomer, tells of the god who found the titaness Necessity wandering hysterically in Chaos and turned her into an ordered and productive domestic. The problem is that such technical ordering, such τέχνη, is bound up with engendering, procreating, and lovemaking, τίκτειν. The thesis of my chapter—and of the entire book—is that the root *tic-*, suggesting lovemaking and engendering, is soon lost in the mighty *tec-* that comes to be inscribed in our techniques, technics, technologies, and architectonics. Even in our architectures. The question my book raises is this: What would happen if we learned to restore the rights of a different sort of making, if we turned our attention to the concealed sources of the technical, that is, to *tic-?*

If chapter 1 begins with the universe and its *archeticture*—spelling it new, by design—subsequent chapters hardly get beyond these things, except in terms of chronology. Chapter 2 leaps to the opposite and more recent end of a tradition in philosophy, moving from Plato to Kant, Hegel, and Heidegger. It tries to describe something like a liberation of space in modern philosophy since Kant, a liberation of space from time, culminating in a new sense of ecstasy. True, the Heideggerian *ecstases* (as he calls them) are reserved for *time,* and at first blush they seem to have nothing to do with the ecstasies of lovemaking. Yet something in the raptures and ruptures of time, as elaborated in Heidegger's *Being and Time* (1927), opens a path to an essentially irruptive and ecstatic space. After Kant, and before Heidegger, it is Hegel, especially in his *Encyclopedia of Philosophical Sciences* (third edition, 1830), who seems to initiate this explosive liberation or dehiscence of space. It is an initiation that, once it has undergone the Heideggerian turn, takes us back to Plato's *Timaeus* and the thought of χώρα, the responsive place, the amorous space, and the ecstatic event that bestow all room.

Yet χώρα, the "mother" and "nurse" of becoming, especially as conceived by Jacques Derrida, is not simply the provider of domestic comforts, of homey rooms and snug spaces. Every home hides the skeleton—or rather, the flesh—in the closet; every home conceals forbidden objects in what Ben Nicholson calls the Kleptoman Cell. Homey space proves to be quite unhomelike.

Chapter 3 therefore offers a series of archetictural sections— rather than a plan or an elevation—of the *uncanniness* of spaces, buildings, ruins, and of our inhabiting yet homeless human bodies. Heidegger is here joined by the obstreperous Freud, whose 1919 *"Das Unheimliche"* sounds a troubling note for architects and philosophers alike. For while it may seem a pleasure to turn from the technical to the tictonic, such a turn invariably takes us beyond the pleasure principle: it implies a loss of mastery, a failure of control, and an openness to the uncanny.

Chapter 4 then turns to three recent thinkers who introduce foreign bodies into uncanny spaces. Such an introduction helps to transform architecture into *archeticture,* in at least three ways:

1. The human body is perceived and felt, not as the Cartesian philosopher-technician's "fresh cadaver," not as Viktor Frankenstein's meat-plus-lightning, but as a *living* and a *lived* body, as "my own" body *(le corps propre).* The sentient body, as the work of John Hejduk shows, occupies a space that cannot be reduced to the mausoleum of Cartesian geometry. This is the perdurant insight of a thinker who has not yet had sufficient influence on contemporary thinking about architecture—Maurice Merleau-Ponty.

2. The living and lived human body can also be experienced, not merely as a perceiver and doer engaged in its projects, but also as a prime instance of *extravagant expenditure,* as potlatch, in the ecstasies of orgasm and sacrifice. If the hyper-Nietzschean thought of Georges Bataille is "against architecture," it is so only in order that we learn to spell it new as *archeticture.*

3. The human body announces itself as being *more than one,* as inherently multiple. It is a body of folds and lips, a body of *woman* in a perhaps unheard-of sense, a sense that is nonetheless as old as Plato's *Timaeus,* a sense that is insistent but by no means essentialist—the sense developed by Luce Irigaray.

No doubt, others ought to be named and discussed here, others who would join Merleau-Ponty, Bataille, Derrida, and Irigaray in their exitus from the Cartesian vault—others, from Nietzsche to Cixous, whom I cannot even begin to list. Yet it is not a matter of lists. It is a matter of breaking up frames of reference, or of rejoining ancient yet still unfamiliar frames of reference, allowing an ecstatic space for something *other* to approach us, a space for something like *archeticture.*

I TIC-TALK
Space, Time, and Lovemaking in Plato's *Timaeus*

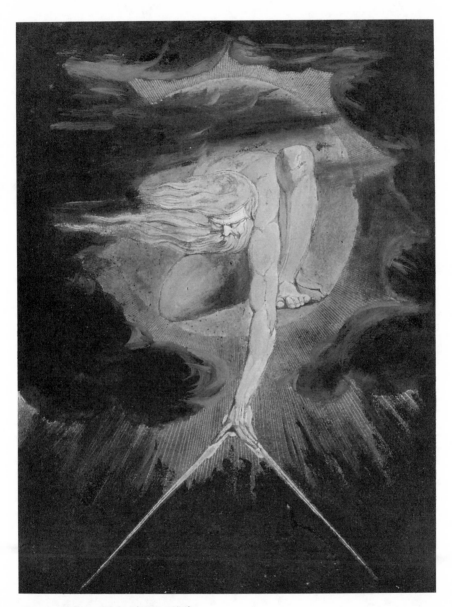

Fig. 1 William Blake (1757-1827)
Europe. A Prophecy, 1794
Bentley Copy A
pl. 1 [Bentley 1]: Frontispiece
Relief etching with watercolor
Yale Center for British Art, Paul Mellon Collection

Necessity's long elevation also resembles an autonomous order.
—Alberto Pérez-Gómez

It is not so much that the pursuit of architectural "being" is
wrong as that it is unbecoming.
—Jeffrey Kipnis

In the beginning of architecture was the ἀρχή, we all know that,
even if some credulous souls continue to confuse the ἀρχή with
Λόγος. Ἀρχή is the ruling principle, the dominant, the commencement that holds sway and governs from beginning to end.
Sometimes it seems as though, in the beginning, the Pythagorean
astronomer called *Timaeus* was able to say it all; as though we ourselves constitute the ends of his multimillennial beginning. The second portion of the word *architecture*, we also know, involves τέχνη, or at least the teaching of the techniques and "technics" of
design, fabrication, and building; the word *architecture* therefore
suggests the governance or ruling sway of all the words in Western

languages that have *tec-* as their root. It is no doubt a personal quirk of mine—a classic hysterical symptom like nausea or numbness in the limbs, perhaps an uncontrollable reflex movement about the perimeter of the eye—that I wish to spell this root new. Not *tec-,* but *tic-.* Not architecture, but archeticture.

Because I had good technical training in philosophy (which is where the architects, with their unparalleled technical training, stand with *their* noses pressed against the windowpane), I was always well-informed about *tec-.* Only belatedly did I learn of the root *tic-,* and through a kind of back door, awkwardly, in the way we learn things at school, trundling oversize books—dictionaries, for example. Liddell-Scott's *Greek-English Lexicon* (1940) contains in its 2,111 pages a few lines about τίκτω, τίκτειν, a few sparse lines of *ticture.* Not *tincture,* especially not a tincture of philosophy, which I would not wish on anyone, but a kind of *archaic ticture.* I do not want to bore my readers with long-winded excerpts from dictionary entries, but allow me a few tidbits, scraps that usually get lost in translation. Whereas Aeschylus writes ὁ τεκών or ἁ τεκοῦσα, "beget-ter" or "sire," and "bearer," respectively, these words are normally translated simply as "father" and "mother" (*Libation Bearers,* lines 690, 133). When in Sophocles' *Electra* Clytemnestra exclaims, "Mother and child! It is a strange relation" (line 770), we are some-how protected from the Greek: δεινὸν τὸ τίκτειν, "Uncanny, over-powering is this matter of engendering!" "Monstrous is this thing we call sexual reproduction!" Sometimes the sense of engendering in τίκτειν is quite general, as in Sophocles' *Ajax,* where we hear that favor *breeds* favor (line 522). Yet most often τίκτειν is explicitly a matter of blood and semen, of houses stained by murders and adul-teries among the ancestors; it is apparently a matter of that small number of very special families, as Aristotle says, that constitute the infamous houses of tragedy. The House of Atreus was built by *archeticture,* not architecture.

Yet the roots *tic-* and *tec-* encroach on each other. The child is τὸ τέκνον, whereas the joiner, carpenter, or master of arts, is ὁ τέκτων. Τεχνάζω, "I contrive or devise," aims at something that is τίκος, "refined, artificial," and almost inevitably gets mixed up with τεκνουργία, the begetting or rearing of children. It is as though our own word "reproduction" were quite naturally and inevitably the odd mix of technics and love life that it is, a mere mimicry of Greek "production." Indeed, the two roots of love and work, *tic-* and *tec-,* are intricately imbricated, even intertwined. Perhaps it is silly to try to muster them into a straight line, to separate out and arrange the lines of their descent, with the x's and o's clearly distinguished from one another: perhaps it is puerile to play tic-tec-toe with them.

However, I wonder—even if it sounds suspiciously like a grand narrative, indeed, the grandest of all narratives—whether in the West we have not always quite relentlessly reduced the one root *(tic-)* to the other *(tec-),* reduced it to the point where we have all but eradicated the senses of engendering and of the love play that may induce reproduction. We seem to be reluctant to concede that after one has made one's bed with technical proficiency one must sleep in it, and that it is after all rather different to sleep with someone than alone. All making belongs in the public domain, all sleeping in the private. We make things, and thus "make it" in the vertical, professional world of drawing tables and stools. If we "make it" on the horizontal, "make it" with someone, we consider it indiscreet to discuss the matter in public; or else, on the contrary, we bandy about such "making it," as though it were a matter within our manipulation and control, a matter of mere technical contrivance and design. Whether we are diffident or obnoxious about it, however, we sense

the subtle difference: it is one thing to be the world's cleverest architect or critic or philosopher, another to love somebody or something
to distraction and despair. (It will therefore not have been paternity
or maternity I wish to talk or write about at all, but something that
such reproduction presupposes.) Freud says that all culture, and not
only in the West, depends on human beings' capacity to busy themselves with *tec,* to rise on the afflatus of what we now call "high
tech," because, deep down where we are all exposed superficies,
we know what makes us *tic.* Yet our "making it" at that ostensibly
lower level has little to do with our adept tinkering and proud pro-
fessionalism, no matter how much we say we love our work.

Does such tic-talk mean to "psychologize" architecture, criticism, and philosophy? If only such psychological reduction were
genuinely possible! However, psychoanalysis (to take one example)
is itself twisted in this regard, its energetics of drives yoked to the
ergics of its own work—the analyst's technical know-how plumbing
the depths and claiming to design a productive therapy.
Professional philosophy is worse: utterly enamored of its own technical wizardry in argumentation, it runs its epistemological vacuum
cleaner roughshod over everyone else's language, scoring points
each time an opponent's ideas can be proven to be either false or
trivial. Certainly, in loquacious philosophy, as in busy-busy architecture, there is no time taken to talk about that other root, *tic-.* No
time for tic-talk.

Let us carve out a snippet of time—and space—for such talk. What
would architecture be like in a world where not everything and
everyone were at the disposal of technical calculation, fabrication,
measurement, and manipulation? Where not everything and everyone were amenable to design? What would architecture be like if

we spelled it new—or very old, as the case may be—as *archetic-ture?* What would things be like in a world where in order to *make* something one had to make it *with* that something, as though making it *with someone?* A world where one would have to be not merely polite but in the

> Our task is to remember that we must remain among the living, among the creators of worlds. Yet we can accomplish this only through the work of the two halves of the world: masculine and feminine. (Luce Irigaray, *E,* 122)

desperate position of having to *beseech,* a world where one would always be head over breakfast in love?

Of course, paternity does not require love. Neither does maternity, with which paternity seems to rhyme. Accident is always a possibility, even a likelihood. Accident, resentment, and subsequent abuse. Nevertheless, even in this time of the New Puritanism, the Right-to-Life, and the Death of Sex, a certain confusion continues to run rampant. People everywhere continue in spite of it all to risk love. Not many risk it in the classroom or design studio, to be sure, but legions take a chance out on the street or in the corners of discreet rooms. The advertising on inner-city buses and elevated trains proves it: two blurbs adjacent to one another on the band of advertisements that grace the cars of the Chicago El, the first proclaiming "Free Pregnancy Testing—No Questions, Answers," the second proffering a cheery "Hi, I'm Bill. I'm learning to live with HIV." Tic-talk, in *our* time?

Such talk would have to allow itself to be complicated by all sorts of things right from the start. Indeed, it would have to become an unpronounceable *kti*-talk. For another root that is relevant to both τίκτειν and τέχνη (presuming it is *another* root, and not the result of a mere Freudian-Abelian inversion of letters) is *kti-*, as in κτίζω, κτίσις, "settling, founding, creating," "creature, creation," but also "building," as in the erection of a temple or sanctuary. The archek-ticture of κτίζω, as employed by the historian Herodotus (4. 46) and the tragedians, does a great deal of work: the word means to people a country, to build houses and cities in it, to plant groves of fruit trees, to erect altars, or quite generally "to produce, create, bring into being." It is the word that appears in the Septuagint whenever it is a question of God's creation or of his creatures. Apparently, the root *kti-* comes from the Sanskrit word *kséti,* meaning "to reside," and *ksitis,* "habitation." *Kti-* or *ksi-* talk therefore puts us in mind of *dwelling.*

One of the complications of tic-talk that I have in mind is that introduced by Martin Heidegger in an essay—familiar to most students of architecture nowadays—called "Building Dwelling Thinking." The middle term is the crucial one for Heidegger, who is trying to *think* about *building* on the basis of *dwelling.* In the course of his reflections Heidegger engages in some tic-talk of his own:

> The Greek for "to bring forth or to produce" is τίκτω. The word τέχνη, technique, belongs to the verb's root *tec.* To the Greeks τέχνη means neither art nor handicraft but to make something appear within the scope of what is present, to make it appear as this or that, in this way or that way. The Greeks conceive of τέχνη, producing, in terms of letting-appear. Τέχνη thus conceived has been concealed in the tectonics of architecture since ancient times. Of late it still remains concealed, and more resolutely, in the technology of power machinery. Yet the essence of the erecting of buildings cannot be understood adequately in terms of either architecture or engineering construction, nor in terms of a mere combination of the two. The erecting of buildings would not be suitably defined *even if* we were to think of it in the sense of the original Greek τέχνη *solely* as a letting-appear, which brings forward something produced, as something present among other things that are already present.[1]

There is something unsatisfying about Heidegger's remarks,

however promising the tracing of τέχνη back to τίκτω may be. He introduces the word for engendering and sex, but straightway reduces it to the ostensibly "original" root *tec-* and its scion τέχνη, reducing the two of them in turn to a cryptic "letting-appear." The invocation of *presence* as the meaning of being, and of presence as *radiant appearance,* does absolutely nothing to prompt our thinking in a direction that would eschew the visualist and manipulatory technics and architectonics that Heidegger himself derides. There is thus something bloodless about Heidegger's complaint, as coy as it is (*"even if"*). It is as though Heidegger, in this "letting-appear," is taking refuge from something, taking refuge from some powerful force or daimon—what one might call *daimon life.*[2] The welcome complication introduced by Heidegger, however, is that tic-talk will have to speak not only of architecture but also of the presencing of the present. *Archeticture,* spelling itself new, will be about the meaning of being as such.

However, at the moment I do not want to write about Heidegger's project. Rather, my orthographic tic wants to take me back to that most ancient tale of paternity and *poietic* craftsmanship, Plato's *Timaeus.*

Timaeus is speaking to Socrates and to two other devotees of the goddess Athena. He says that in the beginning was Chaos, or disorder, and blind Necessity. Never mind where the People's Worker (= δημιουργός) was in the beginning: let there be Chaos and blind Necessity. Timaeus then tells how the

Let us come back to the hitherside of philosophy's self-assured discourse, which advances by oppositions of principle and counts on the origin as on a *normal couple.* We must come back in the direction of a preoriginary realm that would deprive us of that assurance and at the same time demand a philosophical discourse that is impure, menaced, bastard, hybrid. These traits are not negative. They do not discredit a discourse that would simply be inferior to philosophy. Because if, to be sure, that discourse is not true, but only plausible, it nonetheless says what is necessary on the matter of necessity. (Jacques Derrida, *K*, 94)

Demiurge, as a kind of community organizer, brought order into the Chaos, creating the universe as we know it. Here is how he did it. He "looked up" to certain "paradigms" of "being," following their patterns in his constructions of "becoming." (I forgot to mention, or Timaeus forgot to mention, that the paradigms were there in the beginning too: *in* the beginning, *for* the beginning, hence *before* the beginning.) My readers are already impatient with this scarcely plausible story,

The demiurge formed the cosmos *in the image* of the eternal paradigm he contemplates. The *logos* that relates to these images, to these iconic beings, must be of the same nature: merely plausible (29b-d). In this domain we must accept the "plausible myth" *(ton eikota mython)* and not look for more (29d; cf. 44d, 48d, 57d, 72d-e). (Derrida, *K*, 67)

and want to ask where the Demiurge was when he did this looking up, and why the paradigms were "above" him if he was the designer of the universe. F. M. Cornford, the well-known Cambridge classicist, argued that creation myths and cosmogonies always have to tell the story of creation twice, as though trying (in vain, as it turns out) to account for

the stage setting or backdrop that the heroic creative act presupposes.[3] When Marduk slays Tiamat it is in order to stand on her back and—once again, but always for the *first* time—slay Tiamat. Creations take twelve days, not six: six days to fabricate or breathe life into the world, and six days trying to find the shoes you will have had to step into on the morning of that first day.

Perhaps that is the sort of problem not only the Demiurge but also Timaeus himself confronts. For once he has told the tale of the Demiurge's looking up to the "paradigms" and modeling "becoming" on "being," he confesses the need to start the story all over again, and from the beginning. Indeed, this restarting happens twice, though in the end it never achieves a genuine beginning. Each time Timaeus recounts in detail the story of the Demiurge and his fabrication of the world soul and cosmic body, the story of the several generations of lesser gods and the generation of mortal men (that is, mortal males, male men), he winds up saying that something is missing, he cannot find the handle, he lacks the place or space or even the stuff *in which* the paradigms or models can intermingle with the raw materials of Chaos. Timaeus says he needs a mixing bowl, a kind of container or receptacle in which the "originals" can operate on and somehow influence what will become their "copies." The mixing bowl will turn out to be called χώρα *(khôra)*.

Yet where does he find the mixing bowl—is it up there on the shelf with all the other paradigmatic forms and intelligible molds of "being," or is it down here below, where all the other materials of "becoming" are strewn higgledy-piggledy all over the floor? And can the receptacle possibly contain all the molds plus all the material stuff that should go into making the copies?

Khôra means a place occupied by someone, a country, habitation, designated seat, rank, post, assigned position, territory, or region. In fact, *khôra* will always be already occupied, invested, even as a general place, even if it is always distinguished from everything that takes place in it. (Derrida, *K,* 58)

Timaeus very much wants to reply to these questions. The problem is that he has begun by dividing everything into two, with a never-the-twain-shall-meet gesture and attitude—the very attitude and practice of diacritical division that wreaks so much havoc in Plato's *Sophist:* Timaeus draws a hard and fast line between, first, pure and immutable "being," which is invisible and untouchable, accessible to thought alone, intelligibly paradigmatic as such, and, second, the grosser world of "becoming" or γένεσις, the things we can see and manipulate.

How are we to think that which, although it exceeds the regularity of the *logos*, its law, its natural or legitimate genealogy, nonetheless does not pertain, *stricto sensu*, to *mythos?* Beyond the arrested or but lately arrived opposition of *logos* and *mythos*, how are we to think the necessity of that which, granting a place to this opposition, as to so many others, sometimes does not seem to submit to the law of the very thing it *situates?* What about this *place?* Is it nameable? And would it not have some impossible relation to the possibility of naming? Is there something to *think* here, as we have so hastily said, something to think in accord with *necessity?* (Derrida, *K,* 18)

Yet how could the Demiurge "look up" to pure being if it is invisible? To be sure, Timaeus is speaking metaphorically or by way of analogy when he says that the Demiurge "looked up"; we all know that the Demiurge gazed aloft with or in his *mind's* eye; and if someone persists, asking Timaeus which is the original and which the copy, the mind's eye or the paired bodily eyes, that is, vision or mental envisaging, Timaeus will simply refuse to answer. For he is only repeating someone else's story, an old Pythagorean story, which is what Plato too will have been retelling. In fact, Timaeus is quite explicit about it. He says, "I'm only telling a story, and it *probably* happened like this, but you'd have to be a god to be sure."

Discourse on the *khôra* is thus also a discourse on genre and gender *(genos),* and on the different genres of genre. . . . The *khôra* is a *triton genos* [a third kind] with regard to the two genres of being (the immutable and intelligible vs. the corruptible and sensible, which is in becoming), but it also seems to be determined with regard to sex and gender: Timaeus speaks of the matter as "mother" and "nurse." He does so in a way that we shall not hasten to name. Practically all the interpreters of *Timaeus* avail themselves of the resources of rhetoric, without ever inquiring into the matter. They speak quite calmly of metaphors, images, and comparisons.

However, even with the best will and all the patience in the world, we are going to have trouble with Timaeus's mixing bowl, his recalcitrant yet absolutely necessary "receptacle," which eventually will be called χώρα, which in turn will eventually be translated as *spatium,* space. Allow me to reproduce a page or two from the middle of Plato's *Timaeus.* Here is how the Pythagorean astronomer,

Timaeus of Locri, describes the predicament he is in, as he tries to start all over again:

> This new beginning of our discussion of the universe requires a fuller division than the former, for then we made two classes [48e 3: εἴδη]; now a third must be revealed. The two sufficed for the former discussion. One, which we assumed, was a paradigm, intelligible and always the same, and the second was only the imitation [48e 6: μίμημα] of the paradigm, generated and visible. There is also a third, which we did not distinguish at the time, conceiving that the two would be enough. Yet now the argument seems to require that we should set forth in words another kind, which is difficult of explanation and but dimly seen. What power and nature are we to attribute to it? We reply that it is the receptacle, and in a manner the nurse, of all generation.

(Note: The apparent multiplicity of metaphors or mythemes in general in these places signifies, not that the proper sense can become intelligible only by means of these detours, but that the opposition between proper and figurative meaning, albeit without losing its value altogether, here encounters a limit [*K*, 100–101].) They pose no questions about the tradition of rhetoric, whch places at their disposal a stockpile of very useful concepts—but all of them construed on the basis of this distinction between the sensible and the intelligible to whcih precisely the thought of the *khôra* can no longer accommodate itself. Indeed, Plato gives us to understand without ambiguity that the thought of *khôra* has the gravest difficulty accommodating itself. This problem of rhetoric—which is singularly a proglem of naming—is not, as we can see, a merely accessory problem here. (Derrida, *K*, 20–21)

A moment later Timaeus elaborates on this vaguely envisaged and wholly unaccountable "nurse." She—if we can call her that—is of a nature that "receives into itself all bodies." Herself utterly promiscuous—or generous, as the case may be, but in any case capacious—she must always be addressed as *the same*, for,

inasmuch as she always receives all things, she never departs at all from her own nature and never, in any way or at any time, assumes a form like that of any of the things that enter into her; she is the natural recipient of all impressions, and is stirred and informed by them, and appears different from time to time by

One must not confuse *khôra* with a generality, attributing to it properties that would always be the properties of a properly determinate being, that is, of one of the beings that *khôra* "receives," or of one of the beings whose image she "receives": for example, a being of the feminine gender—and that is why the femininity of the mother or nurse can never be properly attributed to khôra. (Derrida, K, 33)

reason of them. But the forms that enter into and go out of her are the imitations of eternal beings, imitations modeled after their paradigms in a wonderful and mysterious manner, which we will hereafter investigate. For the present we have only to conceive of three genera: first, that which is in process of generation;

Who are you, Khôra? (Derrida, K, 63)

secondly, that in which the generation takes place; and thirdly, that of which the thing generated is a resemblance that has arisen naturally [50d 2: φύεται]. We may liken the receiving principle to a mother, the source or spring to a father, and the intermediate nature to a child.

In truth, every narrative content—whether of fable, fiction, legend, or myth matters little for the moment—becomes in its turn the container of another tale. Each tale is thus the *receptacle* of another. There are only receptacles of narrative receptacles. (Derrida, K, 75)

Such is the happy and holy family of the Demiurge: the paternal font, the nascent ordered universe, and the maternal "in which." Timaeus notes that the "in which," the mother, must be shapeless—in order not to impose her own form on her offspring—and neutral, "like the base of a perfume." "Wherefore," he concludes, "the mother and receptacle of all created and visible and in any way sensible things is not to be termed earth or air or fire or water, or any of their compounds, or any of the elements from which these are derived; but it is an invisible and amorphous being that receives all things and in some mysterious way partakes of the intelligible, and is utterly incomprehensible" (51b). A moment later Timaeus sets an impenetrable seal on the mystery of the receptacle, which seems to lie neither on the shelf nor on the floor but to hover in midair, as though she were a great daimon or titaness: we understand her, says Timaeus, only when we leave our five senses out of account, and our lucid ratiocinations as well—only when we enter into a dreamlike state, engaging in a kind of "bastard reasoning" (52b 2: λογισμῷ τινι νόθῳ). Such a dreamlike state opens a space for tic-talk.

The philosophical tradition has often identified "bastard reasoning" as φαντασία, *imagination* or *fancy,* an essential—yet essentially seductive—faculty of the soul. The great Renaissance translator of Plato, Marsilio Ficino, renders the phrase as "adulterated reasoning," but, whether we opt for bastardy or adultery, it is clear even to Timaeus that the nurse and mother of becoming is not only difficult but also dangerous to descry and describe, especially for an expectant father, whose craftsmanship and technique will not help him now that he is going to confront the Mother of Becoming—and perhaps the Mother of Being as well.

Bastard reasoning concerns the mother of the sole *legitimate* son or daughter of the universal father. *Adulterated* reasoning concerns the *only* consort whom the *sole* father of the "monogenic" universe can have embraced. Timaeus needs a kind of illegitimate logic to envisage her, even though she is eidetically unique (and thus on the side of pure "being"), for she is beyond all seeing and touching and thinking. Yet it seems clear that the Demiurge will have had to touch her, and not with his mind's eye. The mother and nurse of becoming is called Ἀνάγκη, blind and fateful "Necessity."

> If the cosmo-ontological encyclopedia of *Timaeus* presents itself as a "plausible myth," a tale ordered upon the hierarchical opposition of the sensible and the intelligible, of the image that is in becoming and eternal being, how are we to inscribe and situate a discourse on *khôra* there? *Khôra* is of course an inscribed moment, but it also turns on a *place of inscription* concerning which it is clearly said that it *exceeds* or *precedes*—in an order that, moreover, is alogical, achronological, and anachronistic as well—the oppositions that constitute the mytho-logical as such, mythical discourse as well as discourse *on* myth. On the one hand, by resembling a thought process that is *dreamlike* and *bastard,* this discourse causes us to think of a kind of myth-within-the-myth, of an abyss opening up within myth in general. However, on the other hand, giving us to think about what pertains to neither the sensible nor the intelligible, neither becoming nor eternity, discourse on *khôra* is no longer a discourse on being, is neither true nor plausible, and thus appears to be heterogeneous to myth, at least, to the mytho-logical, to this philosopho-mytheme that orders the myth in the direction of its philosophical *telos.* (Derrida, *K,* 67-68)

Each time Timaeus has to recommence his story, things get more difficult instead of easier for the father—necessarily so. Why? Because—or so at least it seems to him—blind Necessity is a bitch.

Let us not get upset. Let us—whether we identify ourselves as women or men or some third thing—not be offended if the mother of the legitimate universe is called a bitch, while the father is touted as the best and most generous of benefactors. For *someone* must be held responsible for the slippage that makes becoming or γένε- σις something less than pure being; *someone* must be held responsible for the nameless adversity and inscrutable attrition that causes every copy to be worth less than its original; *someone* must be found or invented who bitches the type, as it were. For millennia hence, and not only in the West, *she* will be held responsible for the slippage or seepage, the adversity and attrition; *she* will be held responsible for the gaping wound or fissure in being. It is as Mary Shelley's monster declares as he bends over the sleeping figure of Justine: "[N]ot I but she shall suffer; the murder I have committed . . . she shall atone. The crime had its source in her: be hers the punishment!"[4] *She* will be derided as that exceedingly ill-tempered breed whom the male man fears whenever he sees the sign on the garden gate: Beware of the Dog.

  Let us not growl. For "dog," at least for a bastard orthography, is a sort of illegitimate Abelian-Freudian palindrome, as "madam" is a legitimate one: spell it backwards and you get (almost) the same word. D-O-G, G-O-D. (I am writing very cryptically, well-nigh theo- logically, and my readers must forgive me that, but I think both they and I see what the Demiurge is beginning dimly to discern and vast- ly to fear—namely, the reversibility of all hierarchies.) The Demiurge is afraid of that bastard palindrome. He hopes it is only a problem

Fig. 2 William Blake (1757–1827)
The First Book of Urizen. Lambeth, 1794
Bentley Copy A
pl. 11 [Bentley 17]
Relief etching, color printed with watercolor
Yale Center for British Art, Paul Mellon Collection

with his spelling. It is not. It is the fundamental problem of *archetic-ture*. And for any master patriarch or male man, archeticture embod-ies a truly pestilential danger, the danger of the utterly uncanny.

Plato, I believe, is asking Timaeus and his Demiurge to sur-render something, to expose themselves to their own limits and limitations, to forfeit their proud inde-pendence, to allow their cocksure confidence to be shaken, to interrupt their absorption in their own expertise. Plato is asking the astronomer to loosen up and laugh a little at himself, to shake off the air of imperious power and know-how that surrounds him. In fact, Plato's *Timaeus* is at times a very funny dialogue, something on the order of a situation comedy. I must concede, how-ever, that for the past two thousand years philosophers have taken it as gospel, without the slightest inkling of its nature as farce.

In this theater of irony, where the scenes are contained in one anoth-er as a series of receptacles with-out end and without bottom, how are we to isolate a thesis or a theme that one would tranquilly attribute to "the-philosophy-of-Plato," indeed to the only philoso-phy there is, which is Platonic? This would be to misconstrue or deny outright the textual structure of the scene, to believe one could resolve all the questions of a gen-eral topology, including the ques-tion of the places of rhetoric, and to believe that one comprehends what it means to receive, which is to say, to comprehend. It is a bit too soon. As always. (Derrida, *K*, 80)

I do not have the time or space to present even the wackiest parts—for example, the parts where Timaeus, who is a leading member of the Pythagorean Brotherhood, explains that in the cycles of reincarnation women are barely one level above dogs and fish, or those where Timaeus tells us all about disease and about the way illness came into this otherwise perfect world, built by design and modeled on paradigmatic being. The last disease he describes is ἀφροδίσια ἀκολασία (86d 3), "sexual intemperance." That disease is communicated to male men by female women, communicated, miraculously, *even before women come to exist as such*, even before the female makes herself available as the receptacle into which wicked or cowardly men can collapse and suffer degradation. A nonexistent womankind injects the men with the very disease that will call for her own introduction into the world. She thus marks the contagion (along with the pusillanimous lust) with which and by which—and even *in which*—men come to exist. Such are the vicissi- tudes of bastard reasoning, the distraught reasoning that quakes in fear before both the bitch and the bastard, before Necessity and all her children. Allow me to reproduce one last passage from the zani- est sitcom of Western philosophy, even though some of my readers are weary of my sense of humor, or of Timaeus's, and rightly so.

Who are you, *Khôra?* (Derrida, *K*, 63)

> On the subject of animals, then, the following remarks may be offered. Of the men [i.e., males] who came into the world, those who were cowards or led unrighteous lives may with reason be supposed to have changed into the nature of women in the second generation. And this was the reason why at that time the gods created in us the desire of sexual intercourse, contriving in man one animated substance, and in woman another. . . . Wherefore also in men the organ of generation becoming rebellious and masterful, like an animal disobedient to reason, and maddened with the sting of lust, seeks to gain absolute sway, and the same is the case with the so-called womb or matrix of women. The living creature in them passionately desires to make children, but when it remains barren long past the proper time it often suf- fers fretful irritation; and wandering everywhere throughout the body, obstructing the respiratory passages, it prevents them from taking in breath, drives the body to the worst extremes, and produces all sorts of illnesses, until passionate desire and love from each side gather together, plucking fruit from the trees, as it were, sowing in the fields of the matrix living creatures that are invisible because they are so small and have no shape, letting them develop there and come to maturity within, and after all this bringing them to light, thus fulfilling the generation of living creatures.
>
> In this way, women and all that is female were made. Now, as for the race of birds. . . . (90e-91e)

The passage is memorable if only for its classic symptomatol- ogy of hysteria. Yet its importance is truly universal. For the wan-

What is said mythically thus resembles a discourse without a legitimate father. Orphan or bastard, it is distinguished from the philosophical *logos* which, as *Phaedrus* tells us, must have a responsible father, a father who responds—for it and about it. We find this familial scheme on the basis of which one situates a discourse once again at work whenever we try to situate, if we can still put it this way, the place of any site, meaning *khôra*. (Derrida, *K*, 90)

dering womb and room of the universe, the mother and nurse of planetary becoming, is itself hysterical. Complete with nervous tic, the hysterical somatic conversion of τίκτειν. Whatever touches her cont(r)acts contagion. Indeed, she does not even need to *be* there for her contagion to spread. It is as though she sprang armor-clad from the head of Zeus the Father as "fretful irritation," cowardice, lubricity, and distress, which of course ought to have made us wonder about Zeus's head. At all events, she makes all the stories falter, and causes the storytellers to begin all over again, and each time they begin it is one more new botched— or bitched—beginning.

Time is ticking by and some or all of my readers are getting increasingly ticked off. Rightly so. What has any of this to do with those who dominate the contemporary architecture studio? I have spent a long time with Plato's *Timaeus* because, frankly, it has spent a long time with us: it is one of the two or three Platonic dialogues that never disappeared from the Western archive, not even after the fire at Alexandria, not even during the barbarian invasions and the ensuing Dark Ages of Europe. Although it existed for a time in the West only in Latin translation, we did not need to have *Timaeus* reintroduced into European circulation via Toledo or Damascus. It was there for Vitruvius to peruse, there for Suger of Saint-Denis and Odo of Metz to ponder. Even if it was not always there in the full splendor of its "archaic, Aeschylian diction" (Wilamowitz-Moellendorff), not always there in the tictonic Greek, Plato's *Timaeus* was available throughout two millennia as the splendid comedy of a cosmic *Midsummer Night's Dream*—no mere sitcom—except that it became our blueprint for a universe, our model for what an architect is, and our schematic for what it means to be a man or a woman. In its august presence all laughter was stilled. The irrepressible Samuel Taylor Coleridge—arriving after William Blake, whom one must imagine laboring over Plato's *Timaeus* daily—came closest to bursting the bubble. He tells us the following about his reading:

> . . . I have been re-perusing with the best energies of my mind the *Timaeus* of Plato. Whatever I comprehend, impresses me with a reverential sense of the author's genius; but there is a considerable portion of the work, to which I can attach no consistent meaning. In other treatises of the same philosopher, intended for the average comprehensions of men, I have been delighted with the masterly good sense, with the perspicuity of the language, and the aptness of the inductions. I recollect likewise, that numerous passages in this author, which I thoroughly comprehend, were formerly no less unintelligible to me, than the passages now in question. It would, I am aware, be quite *fashionable* to dismiss them at once as Platonic Jargon. But this I cannot do with satisfaction to my own mind, because I have sought in vain for causes adequate to the solution of the assumed inconsistency. I have no insight into the possibility of a man so eminently wise using words with such half-meanings to himself, as must perforce pass into no-meaning to his readers.[5]

No doubt, Coleridge's reluctance retains a "reverential sense" even at the moments when all sense is lacking and bastard reasoning runs rampant. When it comes to the reception of Plato's *Timaeus,* laughter is far—even when nonsense is nigh.

Feeling anxious that something is missing from my own account, I too want to start over again, no matter how restive my readers may be. I shall start over under the guise of a summary. Plato's *Timaeus*

One does not begin again at the beginning. One does not . . . find one's way back to first principles or to the elements of all things (stoikheia tou pantos). One must go farther, taking up again everything that, up to now, one felt able to consider the origin; one must come back to this side of elementary principles, that is, to this side of the opposition between the paradigm and its copy. (Derrida, K, 93)

introduces the Demiurge as ποιητὴς καὶ πάτηρ (28c 3) of the universe, the "poet" and father, the maker and begetter of the world. Almost immediately it reduces these two rather different epithets to one, calling the Demiurge ὁ τεκταινόμενος (29e 6), the craftsman. The first reduction of paternity to technique has occurred: for *tec*- is not *tic*-, no matter what either Plato or Heidegger says or neglects to say. From hence, the Demiurge is the master of arts rather than one who for reasons beyond his control desires something or someone and so begets a world-child.

The reduction occurs in a strange context. Timaeus's question is: Did the artificer look to the paradigm of what is always itself, ever immutable, or did he look to the paradigm of the generated? Of course, one will ask how there can be an immutable paradigm of the mutable. However, even if there were such a paradigm, the skilled and beneficent Demiurge would not look at it. No, we are told that he looked to the eternal in order to mimic it—copying the eternal precisely in order to fabricate the temporal, temporary, transient, and changeable. If one wishes to know what sort of master designer looks to a paradigm he or she cannot replicate, or worse, a paradigm he or she has no intention at all of copying, no one will know what to say. Yet doubts concerning the Demiurge's skill as a joiner do not bother me as much as worries concerning his social skills. For, from the outset, wherever Necessity is concerned, the Demiurge is in deep waters.

There are two details about the father's creation of the universe that I want to emphasize. First, the *result* of his creation is a world

Fig. 3 William Blake (1757–1827)
The First Book of Urizen. Lambeth, 1794
Bentley Copy A
pl. 7 [Bentley 12]
Relief etching, color printed with watercolor
Yale Center for British Art, Paul Mellon Collection

that is *alive, ensouled,* and *intelligent.* Not a robot, not a clone, not gasballs spinning about in space, not pineapple rock, but τὸν κόσ-μον ζῷον ἔμψυχον ἔννουν (30b 7-8). The father *engenders* something *alive.* How does he do it? Not merely by looking up and down, you can bet on it. Not merely by sleight of hand or eye. Had he been a figure in Egyptian, Mesopotamian, or Hindu myths, the master of arts would only have had to masturbate. Alas, he was Greek, and needed help. Second, but still expanding on the first, the Demiurge is not alone. Not only are the paradigms outside and above him, but so also is the visible proto-universe already there, wandering in dis-order—Necessity drifting hysterically in and as Chaos. This is what the Artificer has to work with; or, if the ordered universe is to be viviparous, this is what he will have to *love.* As we have heard, she is called Ἀνάγκη. She is blind. She is a fussbudget. But she has got the stuff—the only stuff there is. She has got all the moves, all the matter, and the only rooms. She is an angel, albeit a sort of blue angel, and the Demiurge begins to look a lot like Emil Jannings as Professor Unrat. *Unrat* in German means "filth." What has the archa-ic technician got himself mixed up with? He wants to be the mas-terful architect of the monogenic universe, which will be "one of a kind," and every architect after him wants to be just like him. What is *she* doing here? And what is she *doing* here? And, finally, can she truly be as unintelligent as the Demiurge fears (or desires) her to be?

Ananke is Necessity. The universe "is generated by a cause of something, of necessity" (28c 2-3: ὑπ᾽ αἰτίου τινὸς ἀνάγκην εἶναι γενέσθαι). *Whatever* she is doing here, she and her action are nec-essary. In fact, as we have seen, they are necessary from before the start.[6] The entire Platonic dialogue takes place in the city of Athena—who is intelligence itself for the Greeks—on one of the goddess's festival days (21a). What may pass for mere misogyny in the Pythagorean city of Locri, Timaeus's home city, is blasphemy or high treason in Athens. Moreover, the very first topic of conversation among the men on that day is the proper mix of women and men for the production of babies (18c-19a). Finally, the dialogue ends with a description of Eros, love, and mating between women and men, both of whom have to be more or less present when they do the deed. We believe that Plato wrote this dialogue. Yet either he was a very sloppy writer (*pace* Coleridge) or these tensions and contradictions touching women and "the female in general" are there for a reason. A bastard reason, maybe, but a reason. Perhaps readers of the dialogue, which is really Timaeus's extended monologue, are meant to interrupt the technical, architectonic discourse with a discourse of another kind? Perhaps readers are being asked to open a space and time for tic-talk?

> Philosophy cannot speak philosophically about anything that even resembles its "mother," its "nurse," its "receptacle," or its "surface impression." As philosophy, it can speak of the father and the son, as though the father would engender it all by himself. (Derrida, *K*, 96)

I am uncertain about the kind of discourse my own attention to *archeticture* ought to engender. I doubt whether it can be readily identified with any given feminist discourse, although it is perhaps closest to the webs and wefts spun by Luce Irigaray and Hélène Cixous. Certainly, it does not revert to Plato's *Timaeus* either to reinforce or merely to regret its misogyny. I am uncertain about how such aboriginal misogyny can be countermanded or resisted or even comprehended. On the one hand, is it simply a matter of emphasizing sex and love

> Does the man make himself a place to receive and to have received feminine *jouissance*? How? Does the woman make herself a place to have received the masculine *jouissance*? How? How does one pass from physics to metaphysics there? From the physical envelope of sex to the enveloping of an envelope that is less tangible or visible but that makes place? (Irigaray, *E*, 59)

over technical mastery, and are sex and love to be dumped in the lap of womankind alone? Is it enough to engage in the *romanza* that reduces woman to her "reproductive function" or her "aura" as effectively as the most bitter misogyny does? Is not that what at least one half of our tradition has always done? On the other hand, is it a matter of insisting that women are as masterful as men, that they are equal or superior in *technical* skill? Is it a matter of lowering the pitch of the feminine voice to the metallic nasal baritone of the female newscasters on television—the North American solution, as it were?

In a profession (or two professions, if we count philosophy) where most of the prima donnas are men, it is perhaps offensive for a man to equate the two sets of problems. Yet I wonder whether the prima donna of either sex is prepared to confront *archeticture,* which requires not merely *two* of a kind but always *more than two,* always more than being and becoming, thought and sensation, logic and poetry, the literal and the figurative, calculation and inspiration. Always more than two, always 2 + *n*, always a mix or an open space—an ecstasy—within any given element or participant, always a readiness to swap or surrender identities and prerogatives to something beyond all contrariety and all logics of contradiction. Nothing harder for the master. Nothing harder for the mistress. However, without multiplicity, mix, swap, surrender, ecstasy, and humor—no archeticture. Instead, an architecture shaped in the traditional mold, one that exchanges the entire universe of life for a few facades of power.

In archeticture, as opposed to architecture, it works like this: You might hate the Chaos you find out there, but you still have to negotiate with it, persuade it, ask yourself, am I willing to go even a single step with that one, and will it or she or he be willing to put up with my εἴδη, my ideas, my forms, my paradigms, my bulk, my all-of-me; you will have to be receptive, more than merely civil, bullying will not do any good, and hate has no talent; you will have to ask whether you may, would it be all right if, and you will have to wait for an answer; you will have to exercise all the discipline and authority of the dancer, moving with *grazie*, by grace of grace; not without discipline, but never by dint of authority; and then you will have to ask, is it really happening to us, to all 2 + *n* of us, are we really making it? In short, you will have to get used to life lived out on a limb, a life lived in the limbo of desire, a life lived in the very deep waters of Necessity and the Chaos of the body.

One last thought. Plato's *Menexenus* says (at 238a) that the Earth does not imitate women; rather, women, when they conceive, give birth, and nurture, imitate the Earth. Perhaps both men and women—and even all third things—have to imitate women in this respect, who themselves imitate the Earth, not only in their bearing (in every sense) but also in their intelligence. Presuming that their intelligence is something other than the master's mastery. For no amount of skill ever masters the flesh of the world. Merleau-Ponty says in one of his "working notes" that, even if we are *pregnant* with the perceived world, there never was or is anything like *penetration*. "My body *obeys* pregnancy, 'responds' to it; my body is that which is suspended in pregnancy, flesh responding to flesh."[7]

"My body," whether font, receptacle, or well-formed fetus, "my body" of whatever gender and of all the genders, of multiple genres and untold preferences + *n*, remains "suspended in pregnancy." All we can say, and it is precious little, enough perhaps only for a nascent *archeticture*, is that even if there are no firm grounds or paradigms or identities to stand on, nobody intervenes in midair, either. The figures to which men and women respond, the figures to which they are drawn and with which they negotiate and plead, the figures they silently and ardently desire, are always already there, inchoate but obdurate in their presencing. She—or, for that matter, which is the matter of desire, he, or it—is always already something *else,* always more becoming than being, always more of the *other.* But s/he *is* something else, as we say, and is never unbecoming. The Lacanian grumble concerning the wretchedly infinite, essentially futile, endlessly frustrating chain of the desirous imaginary is certainly one response to this something else—one of the most ancient responses, in fact. Yet there are other responses, other pursuits, less masterful but more dogged, more devoted to tic-talk.

One last afterthought. By the time Augustine pens his *Confessions,* which contains treatises on memory and time, it is clear that the ancient χώρα has been displaced. For all Christendom, the soul is "in a place that is not a place," *loco, non loco.* Henceforth, philosophers will devote their time to the inward journey, through time, toward eternity. Much of modern philosophy confirms the preeminence of time (and eternity) over space (and the sensuous, sensual body). Yet, as we shall see in the following chapter, something of the power of space and place occasionally shatters the hegemony of time, even for those philosophers who are eminent thinkers of time—for example, Kant, who thinks time as the gateway of all our experience; Hegel, who discovers history, as they say, and who sees the progress of spirit as the march of time; and Heidegger, who understands the time of us mortals in terms of what he calls *ecstatic temporality.* For each of these, space returns to haunt thoughts of time, whether they be thoughts of the gateway, the time line, or the ecstasy of human being in the world. Indeed, modern and post-modern thought alike seem to call for something like an *ecstatic spatiality,* which would take us back to Timaeus's predicament and demand of us something like an *archeticture.*

II ECSTATIC SPATIALITY
Liberations of Space in Kant, Hegel, and Heidegger

Fig. 4 Giovanni Battista Piranesi (1720–1778)
Veduta interna del Tempio della Tosse.
Mark J. Millard Architectural Collection, acquired with assistance from the
Morris and Gwendolyn Cafritz Foundation, © 1996 Board of Trustees,
National Gallery of Art, Washington, D.C., 1764, etching

> Should we not resist bemoaning confusion? Should we not
> look for meaning in the complexities and contradictions of our
> times and acknowledge the limitations of systems? . . . When
> circumstances defy order, order should bend or break:
> anomalies and uncertainties give validity to architecture.
> —Robert Venturi

> Self-contradiction, which is what Venturi has in mind,
> is an offense against order.
> —Rudolf Arnheim

Ecstatic spatiality? What is the space of ecstasy or rapture? Liberation of space? *From* what, *into* what? And why should space need liberating at all?

The answers to such questions will not come quickly. Indeed, the subordination of space to time in Western thought—from Plato and Aristotle, through Augustine, on into modernity and postmodernity—is one of the most complex issues in the history of metaphysics.

When we peruse Heidegger's philosophical oeuvre, we notice the prominence of time in his titles, from *Being and Time* (1927) to

"Time and Being" (1961). Yet one of his later essays is entitled "Art and Space," and Heidegger, especially toward the end of his career, worries more and more about the preferential treatment accorded time rather than space in Occidental philosophy up to, and perhaps including, his own thought.

In one sense, the young Heidegger attempts to liberate time from space; that is, to release time "proper," or human temporality as such, from spatial representations of it, representations such as the time line. That line ostensibly consists of a series of now-points strung out along the past, present, and future. Such linear representation of time extends from Aristotle, and perhaps even his Pythagorean ancestors, through Bergson and Husserl. (On Husserl's geometric time line, see the appendix at the end of the volume.) Heidegger's liberation of time from the punctuated time line occurs in his analysis of *ecstatic temporality* in the second division of *Being and Time*.

However, in another sense, Heidegger's career of thought veers from the project of time's liberation from space toward that of a liberation of space itself. For space suffers a kind of suppression, subjugation, and unrelenting subjection to time in modern philosophy since Kant, and indeed in all philosophy since antiquity. Heidegger himself never advances to an interpretation of *ecstatic spatiality*, and this rubric, as far as I am aware, never appears in his texts. Yet I would like to try to advance in the direction of ecstatic spatiality by examining the following themes:

1. The apparent subordination of space to time in Kant's *Critique of Pure Reason* (1781), and the incipient release of space in the second edition of Kant's book (1787).

2. The apparent subordination of space to time in Heidegger's *Being and Time*, and the liberation of space that commences in

Being and Time but comes to full flower only in Heidegger's later work.

3. An anticipation of Heidegger's liberation of space in Hegel's dialectic of space and time in the *Encyclopedia of Philosophical Sciences* (in its three editions, dated 1817, 1827, and 1830, respectively).

4. A highly provisional sketch of *ecstatic spatiality*—that is, an adaptation of Heidegger's existential structures of *time* to a new experience of *space*.

Each of these four themes is intricate, and I can provide only the barest outlines of them here. It is still a matter of reinvoking, or working our way back to, the *choric* space of Plato's *Timaeus*, in order to flesh out the ecstatic space of what I am calling *archeticture*. I

> The *khôra* is *anachronic*. It *is* the anachronism in being; better, the anachronism of being. *Khôra* anachronizes being. (Derrida, *K*, 25)

shall begin anachronistically by leaping well ahead into the second theme—the liberation of space in Heidegger's later work—for purposes of an initial orientation.

In the late lecture entitled "Time and Being" (1961) Heidegger issues a retraction. He recants (no pun intended) the subordination of space to time in his own magnum opus, *Being and Time,* written some thirty-five years earlier. In the 1961 lecture Heidegger says: "The attempt in section 70 of *Being and Time* to trace the spatiality of human existence back to temporality cannot be sustained."[1] The retraction stands as a separate paragraph toward the end of the lecture, and therefore has a strong impact on its readers, who in any case are not accustomed to getting retractions from Heidegger. In the designated section 70 of *Being and Time,* Heidegger tries to show how temporality "founds" the human experience of space. However, the "founding function" of time itself rests on a traditional architectural metaphorics of foundation and construction—in space. In section 70 Heidegger italicizes the following claim: *"Only on the grounds of ecstatic-horizonal temporality is the irruption of our being-there into space possible."*[2] Heidegger's own language disrupts what his analysis wants to say, namely, that space invariably reverts to time in human experience, or is in some way "built upon" time. His own choice of words ("Only on the grounds . . . horizonal . . . irruption [or intrusion, incursion, penetration: *Einbruch*] . . . into space") compels him to admit that language itself is permeated by "spatial representations." He tries to deny the might or potency of space *(Mächtigkeit des Raumes),* but in lecture courses taught soon after the publication of *Being and Time* he concedes the inherently spatial character of all language.[3] To be sure, language is tensed by *verbs* that are alternately present, past, future, and perfect—tensed, in a word, by time. Yet language is also thoroughly *prepositional,* whereby the preposition *in* has a special eminence, as though our being *in* the world, our *in*dwelling, were as significant for our horizons as our temporal existence and all historical occurrences are.

However, we have leapt too far ahead of ourselves. Let us pursue the liberation of space toward ecstatic spatiality, pursue it more systematically, by examining Kant's *Critique of Pure Reason,* Hegel's *Encyclopedia of Philosophical Sciences,* and Heidegger's *Being and Time* in at least some detail.

The Apparent Subordination of Space to Time in Kant's Critique of Pure Reason *(1781; 1787)*

According to Kant, we can have knowledge of objects in the world around us only with the help of concepts in our minds. Yet those concepts, if they are not to be sheer phantasms, must somehow connect up with things in the world as we *receive* them, things that affect our senses and our sensibility, things that enter, as it were, through the portals or apertures of *intuition.* There are two such doors or windows for sense experience, two such "pure forms of intuition": all objects of our *outer* sensibility adapt themselves to the pure form of *space;* all objects of any sense or sensibility whatsoever, whether outer or inner, submit to the pure form of *time* or *succession.* As the word *in-tuitio* betrays, the *inner* sense retains a certain priority: according to Kant, only some objects of our experience are spatial, whereas all are temporal, so that the inner sphere seems to encompass the outer.

> Once again the question recurs: what does *to receive* mean? What does *dekhomai* mean? With the question that takes the form "What does *x* mean?" it is a matter not so much of meditating on the *meaning* of this or that expression as of observing the crease of an immense difficulty: the relation—so ancient, so traditional, so determinate—between the question of sense or of the sensible and that of receptivity in general. The Kantian moment is somewhat privileged here; yet even before the *intuitus derivatus* [derivative, i.e., *human* intuition, as opposed to *divine, creative* intuition] or pure sensibility are determined as receptivity, the intuitive or perceptual relation to *intelligible sense* has always implied, among finite beings in general, an irreducible receptivity. (Derrida, *K,* 61-62)

Yet what about the inherently spatial reference of intuition in the inner sense? *In?* Where? *(Where?* and not just *When?)* Kant explains that time as succession does not pertain directly to the outer sense—inasmuch as time has no *shape.* That is precisely why we need the analogy of the line to represent time to our minds: time "lets itself be expressed" in the form of the line, which is an "outer intuition," hence spatial; that very fact shows us that time is not a concept but an intuition—better, the very *form* of our *receptivity.* The logic here, however contorted, is as familiar as anything we have inherited from antiquity. Let us first hear Kant proclaim the seemingly decisive subordination of space to time:

Time is the formal condition a priori of all appearances in general. Space, as the pure form of all outer intuition, as a priori condition, is restricted to merely outer appearances. By way of contrast, because all representations, whether they have external things as objects or not, in themselves [are] determinations of the mind *[Gemüt]*, they pertain to the inner state. However, this inner state, under the formal condition of inner intuition, thereby pertains to time. Time is thus an a priori condition of all appearances in general, indeed the immediate condition of the inner (of our souls) and precisely thereby also the mediate condition of outer appearances.[4]

Time as succession appears to be the key to the mysterious synthesis of concepts with the aggregate of sense data given in intuition. In the famous "Schematism" of the *Critique of Pure Reason* (*KrV-A*, 138), Kant refers to time as "the formal condition of the manifold of inner sense, and thereby the condition of the connection among all representations." If the "Schematism" treats of a "concealed art," an art that lies "in the depths of the human soul" (*KrV-A*, 141), time is the medium of that arcane art—time, and not space. Music over sculpture and architecture. Kant thus seems to follow a truly ancient tradition, for which the interiority of the mind or the soul is eminently temporal but not at all spatial. As we heard at the end of chapter 1, when Augustine seeks his Father in the caverns of his memory, it is in a *remota interiore loco, non loco,* "an interior space that is not a space."[5]

However, Kantian interiority is not altogether Augustinian, not even in the second edition of the *Critique of Pure Reason,* where the doctrine of "the transcendental unity of apperception" appears to privilege time and subordinate space more strikingly than ever. For in Kant's "Refutation of Idealism," also added to the second edition, something like an inchoate restoration or liberation of space seems to occur, so that the tension between interiority and outer sense increases dramatically. Kant resists the idealisms of both Descartes and Berkeley by arguing that "consciousness of my own existence" depends in a radical way on the "existence of objects in space outside me" (*KrV-B*, 275). Temporal determination as such depends on something *persistent* or *perdurant* (*etwas* Beharrliches) in perception, to wit, a thing outside the mind. Kant elaborates:

> To be sure, the representation *"I am,"* which expresses the consciousness that can accompany all thinking, immediately includes in itself the existence of a subject; yet it does not include any *knowledge* of that subject, nor likewise any empirical knowledge, that is, any experience of it. For this we require, in addition to the thought of something existing, intuition as well, and in this case inner intuition, with regard to which, that is to say, with regard to time, the subject must be determined. But for this to occur, outer objects are absolutely indispensable; it therefore follows that inner experience is itself possible only mediately, and only through outer experience. (*KrV-B*, 277)

The emphasis on the pure form of space and on outer experience continues in the "General Remark on the System of Principles," also added to the second edition (*KrV-B*, 288-94). As Heidegger observes in his book, *Kant and the Problem of Metaphysics* (1929), this waxing emphasis is strange—almost counterintuitive, one might say—inasmuch as the second edition of Kant's *Critique* seems to count more than ever on the spaceless depths of the time-producing human soul.[6] In his "General Remark," Kant insists that if we are to understand *objects* with the help of concepts and categories we still need *outer* intuitions, that is, intuitions of things in space. Thus the famous concept of *substance*—which Aristotle holds to be equivalent to "being" as such, precisely because *substance* pertains to what perdures and thus most properly *is*—relies on our experience of material entities in space. Indeed, says Kant, our inner sense of temporal succession would be a state of chaotic "flux" if it were not for those substantial, material islands in the stream. "But it is an even more noteworthy fact," states Kant, "that in order to understand the possibility of things in conformity with the categories [of the mind], and so to demonstrate the *objective reality* of those categories, we need, not merely intuitions, but intuitions that are in all cases *outer intuitions*" (*KrV-B*, 291). The very oxymoron of outside and inside in "*outer in*tuitions" does not appear to trouble Kant, however much it troubles his system. A moment later in his text he digs the hole even deeper—it is a hole to the outside, an egress for the soul, mind, or interior heart of hearts *(Gemüt)* into the open air of the world: "For space alone is determined as perdurant, while time, and therefore everything that is in inner sense, is in constant flux" (ibid.).

It is therefore hardly strange that Kant should ultimately recoil from liquid time and seek solace in solider space. For there is a profound affinity between Kant's entire *system* of reason and the *space* of a mathematically ordered architecture. Rudolf Arnheim notes the proximity of philosophical system and building, of architectonic and architecture, in Kant. It is a proximity illustrative of the theme of space—as are, no doubt, all proximities. Even if everyone has noted this proximity, Arnheim drives the point home in the final section of his *Dynamics of Architectural Form,* "All Thoughts Take to Building."[7] "When the human mind organizes a body of thought, it does so almost inevitably in terms of spatial imagery." Likewise, when an architect arranges and encloses spaces, he or she does so by thinking of the system of functions that the building must fulfill. Arnheim points to one of the final sections of Kant's *Critique of Pure Reason,* "The Architectonic of Pure Reason" (*KrV-A,* 832ff./*KrV-B,* 860ff.), where Kant treats the "art of constructing systems," which is tantamount to the art of science *(Wissenschaft)* as such. Arnheim interjects: "Although Kant speaks of pure thoughts, the architect will persuade himself that what is here under discussion is his business." Arnheim then cites the second paragraph of Kant's chapter, as follows:

> Under the rule of reason, our cognitions must not be rhapsodic but must form a system, which alone enables them to support and promote reason's principal purposes. By a system I mean the unification of the manifold cognitions under one idea. This idea is the rational concept of the form of a whole, to the extent to which it determines a priori the range of the manifold and the position of its parts in relation to one another. This is to say that the rational scientific concept contains the purpose and the form of the whole, which is congruent to it. Owing to the unity of the purpose to which all the parts refer and in view of which they also relate among themselves, any one part can be missing as long as all the others are known; and no accidental addition can be made, nor can any dimension of the completed totality be undefined that is not determined a priori by definite boundaries. It follows that the whole is articulated *(articulatio)* and not aggregated *(coacervatio)*; it can grow, but only through internal action *(per intus susceptionem)*, not externally *(per appositionem)*, just as the body of an animal does not grow by adding limbs but rather by strengthening each of them and making it better suited to its purpose without any change of proportion. *(KrV-A, 832-33/KrV-B, 860-61)*

It is intriguing that Kant cites the animal body, not the human one, as though only the animal body can illustrate the wisdom of purposeful reason, whereas the human body seems an anomaly or an insult to the architectonic spirit. Arnheim does not pause to reflect on this, but concludes confidently that "all good thinking" can be said "to aspire toward the condition of architecture." Little wonder that when Arnheim meets Venturi, contradiction hits the fan *(DAF,* 163).

The underground river that the soul dreads—the famous stream or "flux" of Heraclitus, into which (as Nietzsche somewhere says) one cannot step even once, much less twice—is the stream of time; it threatens to sweep away the entire project of knowledge and to subvert the entire architectonic of metaphysics. Whereas earlier in the *Critique of Pure Reason* time "could" be "expressed as a line," Kant now writes: "For in order that we may afterwards make inner alterations likewise thinkable, we must *[müssen]* represent time . . . figuratively as a line . . . , and so . . . make comprehensible the successive existence of ourselves in different states" (*KrV-B*, 292). Heidegger is right to wonder (*KPM*, 193) whether *everything* in Kant's *Critique of Pure Reason* would have to change because of this new emphasis on *outer* sense. Space is no longer subordinate to time; indeed, the outer sense now sustains the inner sense. In his own book, Heidegger pays scrupulous attention to the novel importance attributed to space and to outer sense in the second edition of the *Critique* (see especially *KPM*, §§10 and 35). Yet even in the second edition Kant stops short of genuine liberation, and Heidegger himself "leaves open" the question as to whether in Kant's Critical philosophy "space as pure intuition is squeezed out of a possibly central ontological function" (*KPM*, 47).

Can we pose precisely the same question to Heidegger's *Being and Time*? Does Heidegger's own magnum opus perpetuate the squeeze on space? One thing is clear: when Heidegger takes up Kant's project of a Critical foundation for all metaphysics, he too continues to focus on time—at the expense of space.

The Apparent Subordination of Space to Time in Heidegger's Early Work

Heidegger defines *time* and not *space* as the ultimate "horizon" for any sense that the word *being* might have. In *Being and Time* and in lecture courses immediately following its publication in 1927, he tries to elaborate the structure and significance of this temporal "horizon." Borrowing from Aristotle the language of ἔκστασις *(ekstasis)* and from Augustine the rhetoric of *raptus,* Heidegger

Fig. 5 Giovanni Battista Piranesi (1720–1778)
Veduta interna della Villa di Mecenate in Tivoli
Mark J. Millard Architectural Collection, acquired with assistance from the Morris and Gwendolyn Cafritz Foundation, © 1996 Board of Trustees, National Gallery of Art, Washington, D. C., 1767, etching

notes the way in which we are "seized" in the instant of time, indeed, the way in which time leaps ahead of itself and then loops back, suddenly releasing from the movement of future to past what we call "the present," presence in time and space, the presence that has always meant *being*.

However, presence and the present, whether in time or space, are not Heidegger's priorities. His priorities include showing that time constitutes the *animatedness* of our existence. Human existence is essentially *kinetic* and *metabolic*, essentially on the wing, essentially *ecstatic*—not in the sense that we constantly experience joyous rapture, but in the sense that human existence "stands out," is "displaced," and is "cast" or "projected" through time. The *ecstases* of time are themselves *finite*, whether futural (our projection toward a time that is to come, *zu-künftig*), past (our retrojection back onto our own existence as somehow having been always already "thrown" out of a past), or present (our uncertain hold on objects in a meaningful yet mystifying world).

We will have to return to Heidegger's conception of ecstatic temporality in order to ask whether there might be something like an ecstatic *spatiality* implicit in it. For the moment, we have to ask ourselves whether Heidegger's focus on time completely squeezes out or squelches space.

Nothing is less certain than that. For, prior to section 70 of *Being and Time*, where the subordination of space to time is spelled out, only to be recanted years later, Heidegger offers a remarkable interpretation of human spatiality. Indeed, the analysis of spatiality in sections 19-24 of *Being and Time* may well constitute the most radical rethinking of space since Galileo and Newton.[8] The space of *existential* spatiality, the space of human experience, is not pure *extensio;* it is not the space of objects "outside," objects "intuited" through the apertures of the outer sense. Indeed, human being *is itself the outside,* inasmuch as it is always, as Heidegger says, being *in* the world. We are not wan inmates in the gloomy house of detention that is "inner sense," a house with doors and windows to the outside but with bars of subjectivity covering them. Our relation to objects in the world is rather one of use, of getting in hand, hence of approach and withdrawal, nearing and passing by, undistancing and distancing: *Ent-fernung.* (The homology between *Ent-fernung* and the key word for the ecstatic motion of time, *Ent-rückung,* will later become significant.) The existential structure of nearness or proximity, *Nähe,* an intimacy and familiarity that no caliper can measure, is central to both the existential analysis of *Being and Time* and Heidegger's later thinking concerning space. In *Being and Time* it becomes clear that time appears to "found" or "ground" space only as long as we stick to the spatiality of our workaday world and the projects that occupy us from dawn to dusk—for when it is *time* to brush our teeth or leave for work or go to lunch, the *spaces* of sink, elevated train, and beanery magically appear. Or so it seems.

Yet there are several passages in *Being and Time* (*SZ,* 70, 80, 103-4, 211, 413) where all talk of time—which is not yet tic-talk, not yet the talk of embodiment—moves toward a space that is liberated from our daily busyness and our technical projects. As the sun moves through the sky (*our* sky, not Copernicus's), it bestows not only the time of day but also the regions or places *(Plätze)* that things in the world eventually come to inhabit. Sunrise, midday, sunset, and midnight mark not only moments of time but also the inaugural orientations of east and west, north and south. When churches are built facing east, their main portal opening outward to the setting sun in June, and when the graves dug beside the church are laid out on the same axis, with the head of the corpse facing

west, it is difficult if not impossible to say whether time or space
commands the scene. There is every indication that when the fundamental life-and-death possibilities of human existence come into
play the presumed priority of time over space no longer makes any
sense, if indeed it ever did.

Space in Heidegger's Later Thought

In his later lectures and essays, Heidegger often writes about
"time-space" and even "time-space-play." One of the passages in
which time is strangely transformed into the play of time-space is
the following one from "Building Dwelling Thinking":

> Let us think for a while of a farmhouse in the Black Forest, which was built
> some two hundred years ago by the dwelling of peasants. Here the self-
> sufficiency of the power to let earth and sky, divinities and mortals enter *in
> simple oneness* into things ordered the house. It placed the farm on the wind-
> sheltered mountain slope, *looking south,* among the meadows close to the
> spring. It gave it the wide overhanging shingle roof whose proper slope
> bears up under the burden of snow, the roof that,
> reaching deep down, shields the chambers against the
> storms of the long winter nights. It did not forget the
> altar corner behind the community table; it made
> room in its chamber for the hallowed places of
> childbed and the "tree of the dead"—for that is what
> they call a coffin there: the *Totenbaum*—and in this way it designed for the
> different generations under one roof the character of their journey through
> time. . . . (*BW*, 361-62; the emphasis on the words *"looking south"* is mine.)

Reenveloped by this weft of
space-time that she would
have secretly conceived.
(Irigaray, *E,* 57)

Gegen Mittag, literally, "toward noon," is translated here as
"looking south." How "toward noon" can come to be translated as
"looking south" may be understood in the context of the Black
Forest in December: under a meter of snow in the dead of winter,
at about noontime or getting on to midday in that northerly clime,
the sun finally appears in the southern sky over the piney crest of

a hill; when the sun finally appears, its warmth is so intense that you have to open all the windows of the house on its southern exposure; you know both the time of day and your locale in the play of time-space whenever this happens, whether in your journey through time the sun happens to shine on childbed or tree of the dead.

Particularly important for Heidegger's sense of τόπος, *Ort,* or locale—such as the locale of the Black Forest house—are works of art. We would do well to recall some of the principal ideas of the essay "Art and Space" (1969). For if sculpture is the art that Heidegger takes as exemplary here, architecture is nevertheless close by.

Heidegger begins by emphasizing once again that the "space" invoked in his title is not "that homogeneous expanse *[jenes gleich-förmige Auseinander]* which is exceptional in none of its possible sites, is of equal value in each direction, but not sensuously perceptible."[9] It is not the scientific-technological space that submits so readily—so *apparently* readily—to the human drive to mastery and manipulation. As in *Being and Time,* forty-two years earlier, Heidegger associates "space" with the matter of mortals' "fundamental possibilities," especially the possibilities of anxiety and death:

> Space: does it belong among those primal phenomena before which—when we human beings become aware of them—we are, as Goethe says, overcome by a kind of awe, awe to the point of anxiety? For it seems that behind space there is nothing farther back to which space could be traced. In our confrontation with space there is no evasion in the direction of something else. What is peculiar about space must show itself on its own terms. Will it allow its peculiarity to be uttered? (*KR,* 7)

Heidegger takes a clue from the verb *räumen,* cognate with *Raum,* "room" or "space." *Räumen* means to clear the wilderness, to open it up for human settlement and cultivation—for what in chapter 1 we called *archekticture,* on the model of κτίσιϛx. To be sure, Heidegger is thinking not of the destruction of rain forests but of a painstaking nurturing of the locales of human dwelling (*KR,* 9). Yet the two are doubtless related: the shadow of mindless destruction haunts the frontier romanticism of human settlement. When Heidegger goes on to bemoan "the malignancy of homelessness," meaning not the lack of housing but a wretched spiritual condition, we do have to wonder whether the hale and hearty affirmation of homeland, of *Heimat* over *Heimatlosigkeit,* is not the source of many of Heidegger's own problems. (We will turn to those problems at the outset of chapter 3.) At all events, it is the liberation of locales, the freeing up of regions, to which Heidegger wants to gesture, a liberation that would be the principal happening (*Geschehen*) of human history (*Geschichte*). Indeed, history would be the opening up of sites and locales for what Spiro Kostof calls *rituals*—the settings and rituals of something approaching *archeticture.*[10]

Heidegger is of course careful not to interpret *räumen* as a human machination—the expedient arrangement by human beings of spaces that will prove commodious to them. Rather, he points to the "ruling sway" of the "gathering places" themselves, places whose constellated play (*Zusammenspiel*) determines everything about both space and the things in space. Places, locales, domains, and sites gather the things that come to appear within them, gather them in such a way that "the things themselves are places, and do not merely belong in a place" (*KR,* 11). Ultimately, even the empty spaces, the voids and vacuums between and among the things, all the interstices of being, are filled by place and locale (*Ort, Ortschaft*) in the strongest possible sense:

Presumably, emptiness in particular is a sister to the peculiarity of places, and therefore is not a lacking but a bringing to the fore.

Once again our language can give us a clue. In the verb *leeren* [to empty] the word *lesen* [to gather, glean, or read] speaks—in the original sense of the gathering that holds sway in the place.

To empty the glass means to gather it up as the container it is, gather it up into its liberated nature [*Freigewordenes*].

To empty into a basket the fruits we have gleaned means to ready this place for them.

Emptiness is not nothing. Nor is it a lack. In the plastic object, emptiness plays by way of the searching, projective founding of places [*suchend-entwerfenden Stiften von Orten*]. (*KR*, 12)

This place, production of intimacy, is in some way a transmutation of earth to sky, here, now. On the condition that she remember. Alchemist of the sexual, trying to withdraw it from repetition, degradation. Trying to keep it and to make it sublime. *Between.* In the interval of time and of times. Weaving the veil of time, the web of time, time with space, time within space. Between past and future, future and past, place within place. Invisible. Its vessel? Its envelope? Soul of the soul? (Irigaray, *E*, 57)

No doubt the "clearing" of spaces and places becomes increasingly intricate and intimate in Heidegger's thought, and nothing I have written here clarifies very much the "gathering" of things, locales, and interstices within the plenitude of emptiness, the gathering into a searching, projective instauration of space. If we are left with paradoxes and oxymorons, we may find it useful to return to Heidegger's early work on ecstatic temporality in *Being and Time*. However, let me return by way of a diversion—through *Hegel*. For if Hegel does not write in the mode and code of *ecstasis*, he nonetheless knows the necessity of the leap to the outside in both space and time. Hegel constantly senses the suction and seduction of radical exteriority.

Hegel's Dialectic of Space and Time

It would no doubt be perverse of me to focus on Hegel's account of space and time to the exclusion of his detailed remarks on architecture as such. The remarks on architecture occur in his *Lectures on Aesthetics,* and even a brief examination of them reveals why Hegel's philosophy of architecture remains germane to architectural discourses today. Even if the "spiritualist" or "mentalist" framework of the *Aesthetics* appears to have been fractured forever, a comparison of Hegel's account with that of even the most daring of contemporary histories or critical evaluations of architecture shows that our approaches to architecture—our fundamental presuppositions about building and dwelling, our nature and nurture, our rituals and settings, our spaces and sociality—remain indebted to Hegel. No postmodernity can leap over the shadow of its modernity.[11]

If architecture is the oldest of the fine arts, the art in which spirit confronts nature on the "nakedest possible plain" (Melville), it seems to be both the most moribund and the most enduring of the arts. The first to burgeon, its acme or *Blütezeit* is also the first to pass. Enamored of its wood and stone, architecture soon founders under the weight of its own materiality. The truth of architecture is (in) ruins: sculpture, painting, music, and poetry rise from its detritus. In Hegel's retrospect, architecture is subject to the intractable law of gravity; because it seeks a center of gravity in the natural substances of wood and stone, it collapses under the burden of natural needs. Architecture is spirit's knee-jerk reaction to nature, and nature inevitably invades even its most sustained constructions. Hegel calls architecture a *bloß äußern Reflex des Geistes,* a merely

Stone is stonier than it used to be. — In general, we no longer understand architecture; at least, not nearly in the way we understand music. We have outgrown the symbolism of lines and figures, just as we have weaned ourselves from the impact of rhetorical tropes; we no longer suck the mother's milk of this kind of culture from the first moments of our lives. On a Greek temple or Christian church everything originally meant something with a view to a higher order of things: the atmosphere of inexhaustible significance lay draped over the

Fig. 6 Giovanni Battista Piranesi (1720–1778)
Rovine d'una Galleria di Statue nella Villa Adriana a Tivoli
Mark J. Millard Architectural Collection, acquired with assistance from The
Morris and Gwendolyn Cafritz Foundation, © 1996 Board of Trustees, National
Gallery of Art, Washington, D.C., 1770, etching

structure like an enchanted veil. Beauty entered into the system only as a by-product, without diminishing in any essential way the fundamental sensation of the uncanny-sublime, of what is sanctified by magic and the nearness of gods. At most, beauty subdued the terror. However, such terror was everywhere presupposed. — What is the beauty of a building to us now? The same as the beautiful face of a woman without spirit: something of a mask. (Nietzsche, *Human, All-Too-Human*, Part One, no. 218; *KSA*, 2: 178-79)

external and extrinsic reflex of spirit, a ripple passing across the superficies of a mind that is stranded in the desert. And yet.

As Hegel begins to unfold his architectural tale of hollows and shafts, labyrinths and columns, pits and pyramids, and as he begins to tell of the notches and niches carved into the phallic column, a complex fantasia of spirit takes shape. In the huts and temples that human beings build, in the buildings in which people work, leap in dance, sing, perform their ablutions, invent symbols, and achieve the symmetry of classicism and the soaring, vaulting quality of the Gothic, they gather themselves into ever larger and ever more tightly knit religious and political communities. Human beings enframe themselves with architecture in order to open themselves to spirit: *Umschließung,* originally a closing off for protection, is ultimately an *Aufschließung,* an opening onto exteriority—and even onto interiority as such. For closure and aperture alike, by looping back to the inside, express *Geist* or spirit. Thus the dialectical fantasia or, as Friedrich Schlegel calls it, the "frozen music" that is architecture: excavating hollows and erecting columns, nesting in caves and planting freestanding posts and pillars, elaborating decorative tips *(Spitzen)* for those posts and pillars, sometimes truncating them, sometimes raising rounded or pointed arches—all this in some way confabulates the entire story of spirit, even though architecture is only a passing and collapsing moment in the life of spirit.

If we now abandon the even planes and straight lines of the

pyramid, the pyramid pitted with shafts and underground chambers, abandon it for the aridity of mathematical mechanics, that is, *space and time* in Hegel's philosophy of *nature,* it is only in order to examine the interiority or hollow that embraces living gods and goddesses, cradling them as in a basket or tomb. Hegel on the Corinthian column: "A girl of special beauty, so they say, died. Her nurse gathered the girl's toys in a basket and laid it on her grave. There an acanthus plant [ἄκανθος: thorn; from ἄκη, sharp point; hence, acanthus, a thorny plant admired for its leaf] sprang from the earth. Its leaves soon wrapped themselves about the basket, and thus was born the thought of a capital to a column."[12]

Perhaps Hegel's thoughts on space and time, time and space, cannot be thought at all, cannot be brought to the concept. Perhaps they can only be *drawn to* the concept, in all the senses of the phrase; perhaps they can only be drawn precisely in the way the point is drawn to the line, the line to the surface, the surface to the solid.[13] Space and time together constitute "the altogether abstract expanse of being-outside-one-another," *das Außereinander* (*EpW*, §253). (Matter and motion arise as later moments in the unfolding of nature: sedentary stone and climbing acanthus are absent from the primal moment, so that the very relation of architecture in stone or wood to space and time is difficult to conceive, and perhaps impossible even to draw.) However, being-outside-itself, perfect discreteness, immediately falls into two sides, two "forms": the positive form of space and the negative form of time.

Space, although it is "positive form," is the unmediated indifference of nature, the abstract generality of being-outside-itself (*EpW*, §254). As such, it is sheer continuity and contiguity, the next-to-one-another or right-up-against-one-another, *das Nebeneinander.* No particular distinguishing characteristic can obtrude in space, at least not at first. (Is space the nakedest possible plain? Is it a sheet of paper waiting for pen, scalpel or scissors, and glue? Or does the sheet of paper too withdraw forever into a black hole?) Space is mere form, mere abstraction; it is purely external and extrinsic; it is without mediation or midpoint. There are no points-in-space that would be the positive elements *of* positive space: in order to be continuously contiguous, space must be undifferentiated, unpunctuated.

By contrast, the point, which is being-for-itself, is the very negation of space. Space is sheer quantity devoid of quality. (That is the point to anticipate: the introduction of quality: shades of negative form: time. For would not one negate space as soon as the *point* of one's pen or scalpel touched the sheet of paper, as soon as the first timely inscription or incision occurred? Further, would not such a touch be blind, would it not inscribe a memoir of the blind?[14] Would not one have to draw space with an eraser, to unglue it, removing nothing from nothing, in order to find one's way back to nowhere?) For nothing in space encroaches on or disturbs anything else: the *Nebeneinander* is therefore not really contiguity or abutment: the right-up-against-one-another remains asymptotic. "Here" is no place, but the mere *possibility* of place. Space shows no interruptions, no borders, and above all no points of view. Pristine space is a nugatory punctuality: posit a point and you instigate time, interrupting forever a lethargic space, which, taken by itself, is inherently uninterrupted. (Get to the point. Hurry up, please, it's time. Yes, that is the point: get to it.)

The point, in turn, makes sense only to the extent that it is extrinsic with respect to itself and to other possible points. The single

Revising our sense of space. —Have real things or imagined things contributed more to human happiness? It is certain that the expanse of space *that separates our supreme happiness from our most profound misery was produced only with the help of imagined things. Consequently, under the influence of science, this sense of space is always diminished. For example,*

point thus in a way consumes all space and becomes coterminous and coextensive with it. Once one is inside it, the "here" of a point betrays an over and under, a left and right. And yet no "here" within any possible point is ultimate: I can voyage beyond the farthest stars; nowhere is the universe boarded up or nailed down.

the way we learned, and are still learning, to sense the Earth as minuscule; indeed, to experience the solar system as a point. (Nietzsche, *Daybreak*, no. 7; *KSA*, 3: 21)

These thoughts of Hegel's are close to those of F. W. J. Schelling, Hegel's early collaborator, and to those of Schelling's mentor, Franz von Baader.[15] Baader draws the point itself as an occluded circle, or rather, as a *system* of encirclement, involving a movable center and its periphery:

When the center is dislodged or hollowed out and disappears into the periphery (= O), it occasions both universal darkness *and* the solar source of light for a "higher system." The open point is therefore "sun—heart—eye." Were a dark center or *mysterium* to appear

"Place is the primary envelope of that of which it is the place. . . ." (Aristotle, *Physics* 211a). It is difficult not to think of the envelopes of the fetus. The envelope being not to the exact measure of the fetus during gestation, it being her and it (the fetus) besides. They are all in

once again at the heart of the open universe, light would become darkness, or "the sun would be extinguished." That *mysterium* at the heart of a new universe, the center untouched by any periphery, is perhaps better expressed in the tetractys of the decad, the ancient Pythagorean symbol of one, three, four, and ten. Note that only one of the ten

quantitative relations that units (the fifth) is untouched by any side of
shift ceaselessly between the the triangle, floating like a well-formed and
larger and the smaller. . . .
Always, whatever the rap- timely fetus in the surrounding amniotic
ports of the fetus to place fluid of space:
(from the outset to the termi-
nation of its maturation) and
of the masculine sex to the
feminine may be, they pertain to the problem of the
adjustment of the body to the
envelope. Adjusted and separated, what would be the
horizon of the encounter of
the sexes in their different
dimensions? With the rever-
sals of envelopes, and with
envelopments well-nigh to
infinity. (Irigaray, *E,* 49-52)

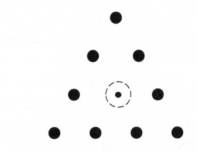

The universe, the organism, and the ego of
a human consciousness can all be
explained, says Baader, by the movement of the center to the
periphery and the leap of the entire point into a new system.
However, any given opening or closure, any O or •, would be as
radically undecidable as it is infinitely repeatable: (•) .

Both the point and the other-than-point (returning now to
Hegel: hurry up, please, it's time) are being-outside-itself: the two
are not distinguished, not separated. Beyond its borders, beyond its
being-otherwise, continuous space is still itself all by itself *(noch bei
sich selbst).* The discrete and the continuous perdure in their unity.
Such is the objectively determined concept of space, space as
abstraction, albeit not as absolute; for space awaits its truth, which
is to be a material mass in motion.

Meanwhile, space is not a box. It is absolutely soft, offers no
resistance. (☞ You cannot point to *[aufzeigen]* a space that would
be space-for-itself; space is always filled space, always a plenitude;
and space is never distinguished from its filling.) Space is therefore

a nonsensuous sensible and a sensuous nonsensible, as Timaeus long ago, in his own bumbling way, said. Things of nature reside in space, and space remains their fundamental position and foundation, their *Grundlage*, because nature is fettered to externality. Space is nature's way of confessing its bondage to things extrinsic.

> The limit of the enveloping body can be understood in terms of the matrix. If it has no exterior, desire tends toward the infinite. Thus the desire of God, who does not know the exterior of the universe? (Irigaray, *E*, 55)

A bondage that is a bandage, a cincture, a cerement of the grave, indeed, a shallow grave scraped into the superficies of an arid wasteland. (Could one draw or erase this space, perform bricolage on or dismantle this space, create or conjure this space here and now? Could one show this abstract continuous utterly undifferentiated nonsensuously sensible space? If one cannot, perhaps the next section of Hegel's *Encyclopedia* [*EpW*, §255] will open some new dimensions?)

Space eventually betrays (but when? at what point in time? has it not already happened?) distinctions within it. First, *immediate* distinctions within its very indifference, to wit, the three dimensions. To be sure, no geometer can deduce the three and only three dimensions of space. There is as yet no point from which one might distinguish length, width, and depth; no direction, no orientation, no *sens*. The Earth has as yet no center, no midpoint, no core. And yet.

There eventually comes to be (but when? again, must it not have already happened?) another sort of distinction concerning space, a determinate, qualitative distinction: the negation of space as an undifferentiated being-outside-itself: finally, yes, we are getting to the point (*EpW*, §256). Such a timely qualitative negation of space is of course itself spatial, inasmuch as every point is a point *in* and *of* space. The point is essentially the self-relation of space, drawing out the space of a rapport. Hegel calls it *eine Be-ziehung*, an active (or perhaps middle-voice) drawing. As space preserves itself in the point, it also cancels itself: the point becomes the line, the first *being*-other of the point. (When you finally get to the point, that is, by the time you will have gotten to the point, there will already have been the time of the line.) Yet the truth of this being-other, the truth of the movement from point to line, is the negation of a negation: beyond point and line alike soars the plane surface, reconstituting the spatial totality as soon as it embraces the negative. For the plane surface is an encompassing superficies that rises and falls in three dimensions in order to isolate a particular space within it: the first solid, the pyramid looming out of the trackless sands. Such encompassing, *das Umschließende*, we recall, is Hegel's name for the primordial effect of architecture, not only of the pyramid but also of the hut, and perhaps even of the temple and cathedral.

Note that the line does not *consist of* points, nor the surface of lines, nor the solid of planes. The line *is* the point as being-outside-itself, that is, as drawing upon space, preserving and annulling itself at once. The plane likewise *is* the line that draws upon or relates itself to space, and so on. If the point is normally represented as first and foremost in the system of space, as the "positive" moment of "positive" exteriority, the reverse is equally true, as Baader and Schelling knew: the enclosed space of the solid is itself the positive moment, first and foremost, the plane surface being *its* first negation, the line its second, the point being the final negation, the one that both draws upon itself and pulls all space back into itself. Punctilious spirit here confronts the necessity of transition *(die*

How to elaborate the problematic of place in such a way that there would not be the cut, the annihilation there, but a becoming by scansion in the relation to place? Return to self in order to depart once again toward the other? Reception in order to rediscover the tension-towards, the expansion. . . . (Irigaray, *E*, 48)

Fig. 7 Giovanni Battista Piranesi (1720–1778)
Piramide di C. Cestio
Mark J. Millard Architectural Collection, acquired with assistance from The Morris and Gwendolyn Cafritz Foundation, © 1996 Board of Trustees, National Gallery of Art, Washington, D.C., 1761, etching

Notwendigkeit des Übergangs), the need for point to leap into line, line to spread as plane, and plane to inflate or conflate as solid, so that the voluminous solid can yield matter-in-motion. At the level of mere representation, the point itself seems to move, even to irrupt as a prime globule of glutinous matter, trailing an attenuated thread in its wake. Or, reversing the motion, the line seems to retract to the single point from which oogenesis commences. Other geometric deductions follow from this: the triangle as the first straight-line figure, the triangle and the square as primary figures or drawings, inasmuch as *Be-ziehungen* (acts or events of drawing) produce *Zeichnungen* (drawings or sketches). That the shortest distance between two points is a straight line is not a synthetic judgment a priori (*pace* Kant) but an analytic judgment: straight line = simplicity of direction = minimum quantity = shortest path.

In the addendum to section 256 Hegel notes that the curved line, arc, or circle occupies two dimensions of space, and that it thus represents the "second power" of the line. The surface that negates such a line would still have only two dimensions, however, frustrating the Möbius strip (which of course produces no solid) before it leaps and curves back to its points of origin. A rather perfunctory account of Euclidean geometry now follows, in which it nevertheless becomes clear how important geometric deduction and reduction are for philosophical conceptuality—for "totality," "unity," and "concept" as such. In a word, for "system," including systems such as Hegel's. For the circle is the place (*der Ort*) of both triangle and square: the philosophers' stone—or the philosophers' delusion.[16]

Postulates
Let it be granted,
1. That a straight line may be drawn from any one point to any other point:
2. That a terminated straight line may be produced to any length in a straight line:
3. And that a circle may be described from any center, at any distance from that center.
— Euclid, *Elements*

Fig. 8 Matthias Merian, the elder (1593–1650)
Construction of the philosophers' stone, ca. 1617
The construction of the philosophers' stone was engraved for Michael Maier's
Atalanta fugiens, an alchemical compendium published in Oppenheim in 1617.
Not all is going well for the construction of the stone: note that the apex of the
triangle that encapsulates the squared circle of man and woman does not touch
the outermost circle of the diagram—if only because of the patchwork ruin of
architecture upon which the construction is being carried out. Something even
more disconcerting happens with the translation of "philosophers' stone" from the
Latin *lapis Philosophorum* into the German. Whereas the German should read *der
Stein der Weisen,* it reads *der* Schein *der Weisen. Der Schein* means "semblance,
mere appearance," so that Maier's German text says: " . . . and you shall have the
semblance of wisdom" (Emblema XXI, *De secretu Naturae,* pp. 92–93). It is as
though Maier had dictated his text to an amanuensis who was hard of hearing
and mistook *Stein* as *Schein,* which is perhaps the fate of all otherwise perfect
philosophical or architectural systems.

We are by now out of space. (Hurry up, please, it's the *nega-tive* moment of being-outside-itself, to wit, *time* [*EpW,* §257], which, let us hope, will move more quickly.) The negativity that relates itself as a point to space, or a point that draws upon space, is time, time born *at* the instant, *in* the instant, *as* the instant when the point consumes all space. Not in one gulp, as it were, but by unfolding or developing in space all the determinations of line, plane, and solid; developing them in the sphere of being-outside-itself, but now also as *for itself.* The point sucking in the soufflé of space for itself also posits its determinations in the sphere of being-outside-itself; yet it does so "simultaneously," "at the same time," *aber zu-gleich,* as time. Time thus appears to be indifferent to the tranquil expanse of the next-to or right-up-against-one-another, the well-nigh contiguous. Indifferent to the lassitude of space, however, time is persistent, insistent. For, as Kant had almost come to see, every-thing persists in space, as space itself persists through time. Even the negations of space, which constitute the reign of time, collapse in "indifferent persistence." Space thus becomes its own "inner" nega-tion, the self-cancellation and self-preservation of its developmental moments. Space, as Borges might say, in time becomes the *aleph.* The existence or *Dasein* of this continuous process *is* time.

In time, the point comes to have its actuality. Space ceases to be indifferent; it now grows restive, is "no longer paralyzed," and is thus already time, already the *difference* that is the negative in itself. Time: the negation that draws upon itself, relates itself to itself, draws itself back or up to itself, *die sich auf sich beziehende Negation.* (The sudden leak in space's plenitude: the nervous tic about the heretofore unblinking eye, the unexpected loop in the lazy line, the restless ripple across the torpid surface, the imploding solid, the sudden rush of wind.) The negative never fully attains its rights in space, which is too full of itself to care. The truth of space is therefore time. It is not we who pass over from space into time, but space itself passes over. Space, and *also* time? Hegel replies: "Philosophy battles against this 'also.'"

Time is existence, the being of a space that somersaults beyond itself. It is the being that, insofar as it is, is *not,* and insofar as it is not, *is*.[17] Time is thus intuited becoming. Further, time is the abstract subjectivity that is born of space's abstract objectivity. No time without the ψυχή, says Aristotle, and Augustine and Kant confirm it. Time is the selfsame principle as the I = I, says Hegel. However, subjectivity here persists in its most extrinsic and abstract form; it is a becoming that is a coming-out-of-itself, a debutante becoming that is almost as continuous as lapidary space itself. Time exhibits no "real" difference, even if it is titanic, even if it is Kronos giving birth to all the world's children and devouring them at once. Time, says Aristotle, citing the Pythagorean Paron, is stupid. (Kronos, who castrates his father, is himself the father of a castrating son, Zeus; if Kronos were smart he'd be dangerous.) Perhaps that is the difference that is eventually introduced by Heidegger: Heidegger is convinced that neither space nor time is stupid, however stupefied we ourselves may be when we think about them.

In Hegel's view, the finite is fortunately transitory, the temporal merely temporary: there is an absolute outside of time, which, however, is not the mere reversion to space. (Yet how can the outside of time be anything other than the *spacing* of time itself?) The proper, absolute outside of time is the concept, *der Begriff,* and the entire machinery of logic, of philosophical *power* and its vaunted *freedom,* over which stupid time has no sway. (Yet, to repeat, how can such conceptuality, power, and freedom—after Hegel—ever be thought as anything else than space and spacing?) The absolute negativity and freedom of the I = I is the power of spirit over time: "Therefore, only the natural is subject to time, inasmuch as it is finite; by contrast, the true, the idea, is spirit, is *eternal* —" (*EpW,* 9: 49-50). And in the addendum: "The idea, spirit, is above time . . ." (*EpW,* 9: 51). Above?

The absolute "beyond" or "otherwise" that is eternity, eternity "above," leaves us bemused as to *why* and *how* individual existence, as *spirit,* "falls into time." Unless that "fall" is always experienced as a drawing of space into time, a *spacing,* a drawing-into and out-of relation between time and space, the ultimate effacement of inside and outside in the system of point, line, surface, plane, solid, and circle. When spirit "falls" into time, when human being commences, the doldrums of eternal space are ripp(l)ed by the winds of temporalizing time. Spirit's "fall" is an ecstasy.

Ecstatic Spatiality

Let us now briefly review Hegel's account (in *EpW,* §259) of the three dimensions of time, recalling only that the *transition* of future into present, and present into past, is always for Hegel a transition in and of *space.* Doldrum or wind, eternity or time, it is always the same sky and sea. Past and future, as negations of the now-point, are quintessentially spatial; they are space itself at the two points— the bivalves—of its passage into and out of time. It is thus impossible to say which temporal dimension yields the other: from one point of view, the past is Hades or the

> There is a terror and a fierceness. The apocalyptic vision of Turner's seas and skies at least were comprehensible, there was a sea and a sky. (John Hejduk, "The Albatross Screeched")

underworld, the seedbed from which nature grows and the riverbed upon which history flows; from another, the future appears as the tireless font of the present and the eventual past. The only "positive"

assertion Hegel can make about the dimensions of time paraphras-
es Aristotle's classic formulation: "Only the present *[Gegenwart]* is,
before and after are not; but the concrete present is the result of the
past and is pregnant with the future." And this bizarre supplement
to time's pregnancy: "The truly present is therefore eternity" (*EpW*,
9: 55).

In Heidegger's view, which is the view that will concern us for
the remainder of the chapter, the dimensions of time are *equally
original,* each one springing from and yielding all the others. Yet
there is no supplementation of the present by an eternity that would
prevail absolutely beyond time. The finitude of time, the finitude of
being, the finitude of human existence—these are not indications of
time's stupor, for which eternity would be the bracing tonic. Perhaps
we should recall the following words from Heidegger's *Being and
Time* before we accept too quickly Hegel's account of a spiritual
"fall" into time: "The problem cannot be: how does 'derived,' infinite time, 'in which' what is at hand comes to be and passes away,
become original, finite temporality; rather, the problem is: how does
*in*appropriate temporality spring from finite temporality proper, and
how does inappropriate temporality, *as in*appropriate, temporalize
a *non*-finite time from finite time?" (*SZ*, 330-31). Every reference to
"eternity" itself tempor(al)izes in time, and is therefore "derivative"
of time. Heidegger accordingly rejects what Merleau-Ponty too will
deride as "the hypocritical sentiment of eternity," which feeds on the
very time it vilifies as stupid.[18]

Like Hegel, Heidegger descries a radical exteriority in time:
human existence *is* its time in the world, a time and a temporalizing
into which humanity does not "fall" but *into* which and *as* which it
is "thrown." As in the case of Hegel, time for Heidegger is *Dasein*
or existence. However, for Heidegger, existence is *care,* a taking-

trouble concerning oneself that is troubled by the possibility that is
most its own—its mortality. What is most proper to existence, its

However, we are perhaps
already in a place where the
law of the proper no longer
makes any sense. (Derrida, K,
51)

time, does not properly belong to it as its
property. In an early lecture course at
Marburg, Heidegger emphasizes that what
most properly *moves* or *animates* exis-
tence is not at all proper to it.[19] Somewhat later, he comes to see
that *time* is what animates us. Even if, following Aristotle, the self
prefers to define itself as a self-moving creature, its projection upon
possibilities in time is hardly of its own doing. What is most proper
to *Dasein* is its persistent expropriation. Its animation is in fact a
kind of ecstasy, a standing out there in the spaces of the world, a
being moved by the raptures or seizures of time. And of space?

Heidegger describes the motion of these raptures or seizures
as *Entrückungen:* removals, transports, sudden tropisms. Whither?
To the outside of any and every atomic "self." "Temporality is the

In order for man and woman to
encounter one another, each must be
a place, but also appropriated for and
to the other, and a place toward
which he or she would be transport-
ed. (Irigaray, E, 46)

original 'outside itself' in and for
itself," says Heidegger, in a complex
and paradoxical retort to Hegel's
point of space-time. Timely human
existence is the ἐκστατικόν, "that
which stands out," pure and simple.

The ecstases of time are three, as are the traditional dimensions
of time:

1. Human being lives out ahead of itself, always already inhabiting the possibilities and projects that come toward it as its own
future. Heidegger takes what is to come, *das Zu-künftige,* quite literally as the coming-toward-itself of existence as possibility-being.

2. Human being is always thrown back upon itself as being
already in a world, as *having-been* always already there. Heidegger

Fig. 9 Giovanni Battista Piranesi (1720–1778)
Avanzi d'un portico coperto, . . . da Roma su la via di Frascati
Mark J. Millard Architectural Collection, acquired with assistance from the Morris and Gwendolyn Cafritz Foundation, © 1996 Board of Trustees, National Gallery of Art, Washington, D.C., 1766, etching

drops the traditional designation of the dimension of the "past" and insists instead on the perfect tense of *Gewesenheit,* "having-been."

3. Human being finds itself by, among, or alongside beings in the world, things that are at hand or on hand for it, items that are "present" to it. Thus the present, *Gegenwart,* is the third ecstasy of time, pregnant not with eternity but with the world.

At times Heidegger seems to derive one *ecstasis* from another, most often electing the future—the "tireless font," as we heard Hegel call it—as the source of having-been and present: "Having-been springs from the future in such a way that the future which has been (better, *is* as having been) releases from itself the present" (*SZ,* 326). The present ecstasy of time would be the egg that is dropped by the future, as existence loops back upon itself, heading toward its own having-been.

At other times Heidegger emphasizes the equal originality *(Gleichursprünglichkeit)* of the three temporal ecstases. Each somehow engenders the other two; each somehow plays out all three *ecstases* in its one: "Temporality temporalizes completely in each *ecstasis.* That is to say, the totality of the structural whole of existence [i.e., the future, the to-come], facticity [i.e., having-been], and falling [i.e., the present], that is, the unity of the structure of care, is grounded in the ecstatic unity of any given complete temporalizing of temporality" (*SZ,* 350). Such ecstatic unity (in a later lecture course Heidegger calls it an "ecstematic horizon" [*MA,* 269]) constitutes the very opening or openedness of human being *along with* its closure and finitude, its being in the clearing of a world, yet always in motion toward its own ineluctable end, its own ruination.

Within the ecstatic unity of temporality, within any given ecstematic horizon, how does one *ecstasis* engender or "drop" another? And how does such a littering of *ecstases* differ from Hegelian spirit's "fall" into time?

What Heidegger most wants to understand is the sudden metabolism of time, the rapid removal or transport from one *ecstasis* to another. When Aristotle describes the "sudden" or "instantaneous" aspect of time,[20] the aspect that Schleiermacher translates as *der Augenblick, das Augenblickliche,* the "moment" or "instant," literally, the "blink of an eye," he creates the very vocabulary of Heidegger's *existential, ecstatic* analysis of temporality:

> The term *suddenly* [or *instantaneously:* ἐξαίφνης] refers to what has departed from its former state [ἐκστάν] in an imperceptible time . . . ; but all change [μεταβολή] is by nature a sudden departing [ἐκστατικόν]. In time all things come into being and pass away, for which reason some called it the wisest, whereas the Pythagorean Πάρων called it the most stupid, since in it we also forget; and his was the truer view. It is clear then that in itself time must be . . . the cause of corruption rather than of generation. For change in itself is a sudden departure [ἐκστατικὸν γὰρ ἡ μεταβολὴ καθ' αὐτήν], whereas it is only accidentally the cause of becoming and of being.

Heidegger agrees with Aristotle and Hegel that temporality is a sudden departure or displacement to the outside, a radical and precipitate externalization. Indeed, such temporal displacement is (if one may say so) a dispersal that finds no eventual haven in heaven. Heidegger resists the view—the view that perhaps makes metaphysics what it is—that time is the merely transitory alienation of soul or spirit, the unhappy sojourn, the temporary inconvenience, the brief interruption of a glorious spiritual program. He tries instead to follow the rapid movement of this temporal "cast" or "throw" of temporalizing existence:

> The phenomena of the *toward . . . , back onto . . . ,* and *by* [or *alongside*] . . . , reveal temporality as the ἐκστατικόν as such. *Temporality is the*

original "outside itself" in and for itself. We therefore call the designated phenomena of future, having-been, and present the *ecstases* of temporality. Temporality is not, prior to that, a being that merely steps out of *itself;* rather, its essence is temporalization in the unity of the *ecstases.* (*SZ*, 329)

When in *Being and Time* Heidegger feels he has to translate the word ἔκστασις into the vernacular, he calls it *Entrückung*, removal, rapture, or sudden transport. The word is structured precisely in the way that the principal word for *spatialization* is structured, and even shares the identical prefix: *Ent-rückung* is by no means remote from *Ent-fernung*. Indeed, one might rather conclude that *ecstatic temporality cannot be thought apart from ecstatic spatiality.* Just as distancing and undistancing, withdrawing and drawing near constitute human space, or "spacing," so does the animatedness of human existence, in rapid and redoubled motion, constitute human time. *Ent-rückung* suggests a sudden jerking or rocking motion, a "start"; it is a motion forward and back at the same time, if such a thing is conceivable. It is perhaps perceptible, *barely* perceptible, in the videographic technique of *pixelation,* the computerized imposition of multiple images in a single frame, producing the sense of a hyperbolic and even diabolic being in the world—Francis Ford Coppola's "Dracula" advancing through the garden at Lucy's estate.

The *-rück* of *Entrückung* has the word *Ruck* as its root: a rapid "rocking" motion, a "start" or sudden displacement, usually as the result of some impact, some pushing or shoving, a "yank" or a "shock." Even when the motion is regular and predictable, the result of the motion may be swift and deadly. The sweep hand of a watch *rückt* toward a particular point in time, say, the instant of detonation in a time bomb. Once again it is Hegel who perhaps in spite of himself gives us something ecstatic to think about: in an early work, written in Jena in 1802-03, he describes the *movement* from natural life to ethical or community life, that is to say, the transition from nature to history proper, in terms of a *Ruck*. For Hegel, the movement from one "power" or "potency" *(Potenz)* of spirit to another, the movement of historical transition that will later be called "dialectical," is anything but a tedious and readily predictable teleological or evolutionary progression. The words "leap," "jump," "shock," and "detonation" better describe such ecstatic-historical change:

> Just as a bomb at the point of its culmination experiences a sudden tremor *[einen Ruck tut]* and then reposes an instant in that tremor, or just as heated metal does not soften gradually as wax does, but suddenly bursts into molten flux *[auf einmal in den Fluß springt]* and lingers in such flux—for the phenomenon is in transition to its absolute opposite and is thus in infinite transition, so that this *exitus* of the opposite out of infinity or its nothingness is a leap *[ein Sprung]*, and the existence of the configuration in its nascent force is at first for-itself before it becomes conscious of its relation to something foreign—thus a waxing individuality experiences the felicity *[Freudigkeit]* of that leap as an interval in which it enjoys its new form, until it gradually opens itself to the negative, and then suddenly finds itself in decline, in diffraction *[in ihrem Untergange auf einmal und brechend]*.[21]

If we ever had the impression that Hegelian dialectic was a staid and steady advance toward the absolute, we will be amazed by this account of catastrophic change. Hegelian history is not easy in the saddle, not out on a romp. Hegelian history is the *Ruck*—the bomb and the breach, the explosive leap of joy, an interval of sudden pleasure, and an eternity of rapid decline. The space of such history is ecstatic, and the mechanism of its movement high speed. But to return now to Heidegger.

How would one draw or collage or build such a mechanism, a device that tosses us simultaneously fore and aft so rapidly that it does not disturb the slumber of our everyday existence? The contrivance that propels us through sleep and waking, in boredom and enthrallment, from birth to death? Heidegger tries to draw it several times himself—even though drawing is not his gift and graphic illustrations are exceedingly rare in his work. In one illustration he shows how the *ecstasis* of the future, on its way to becoming having-been, drops or yields the present. Yet the present, and its "drop," are enigmatic, to say the least:

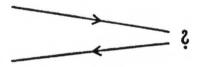

The future descends from upper left to lower right before it suddenly drops the present, the present being the curvaceous question mark. The horizon of the present "remains open," says Heidegger (*MA*, 266): the lines of future and having-been do not converge upon a single point that would be "eternity," "the true self," perdurant "presence," or "full being." They open instead on a point of interrogation.

Such sudden aperture speaks in the Latin word *raptus*, translating ἔκστασις or *Entrückung:* seizure, epileptic access, sudden removal and transport, erotic enchantment and entrancement. Ecstatic temporality is, to repeat, the "original outside itself."[22] Heidegger stresses the fundamental "openness" of such transport. It is indeed an openness of the periphery ( ) that can never crystallize to a definitive horizon O or to a point •, an openness therefore that eludes the idealistic systems of center and circumference ⊙.

A second effort (*MA*, 266) to illustrate or visualize the temporalization of time—an effort inspired by Henri Bergson—is as misleading as it is helpful:

For the scroll that has two spools spinning at a steady pace hardly represents ecstasy. Ultimately, the time of such a scroll is punctual and punctuated. However, no punctuality of the line can serve as the source point or end point of temporalization. Heidegger's quasi-Ionic (no longer, or not yet, acanthian and Corinthian) illustration shows that the future and having-been are intimately related; yet by suggesting that the future is depleted as more and more of its parchment rolls onto the spool of the past, the illustration deceives us. What Heidegger wants to illustrate is the fact that "my having-been 'is' only in and through the way in which the future temporalizes" (*MA*, 267). The arrows of the diagram would periodically have to reverse their direction, and as rapidly as possible; impossibly, the scroll would—perhaps through pixelation—have to ravel in both directions at once. Any diagram or construction of temporalization would have to show the *élan* or *Schwingung*, the rapid, rapturous *oscillation* of time.

Ironically, the illustration that seems to work best is one that Heidegger draws in order to illustrate Schelling's conception of the itinerary of God—God being the tendency inward to the "ground" of the self that is rocked periodically to the outside and thus cast again and again into ecstatic "existence":

Admittedly, it is difficult to tell from Heidegger's account whether the motion proceeds from top to bottom or bottom to top; that is, whether the tendency of (divine) existence is toward greater concentration and punctuality (reading from the top down, on an itinerary of an ever-narrowing narcissism) or toward broader horizons, waxing complexity, and ever-longer leaps to the outside and into the world (reading from the bottom to the top, on an itinerary of enhanced dilation and expansiveness).[23]

If one is to try to *draw* ecstatic temporality, as Hegel would insist we must, inevitably fashioning it as an ecstatic *spatiality*, one might picture it as an existence that ventures into a rough sea, advancing—indeed, thrown—against the force of the breakers, retreating and yet surging forward in the undertow, rocked by the force of the waves themselves:

No doubt, I would be better advised to leave the drawing to others—if not to the architects, at least to archetics and artists such as Piranesi or Ben Nicholson. If I were to depict ecstatic spatiality in words, they would be the following, unfortunately as cryptic as Hegel's and as confounding as Kant's, without being as suggestive as Heidegger's.

> Fools rush out where angels choose to tread. (John Hejduk, "The Albatross Screeched")

It is not enough *to draw* ecstatic temporality and so by a mere ruse of graphics to transform it into ecstatic spatiality, as though such an "automatic" or "graphematic" transformation were straightforward or guaranteed: both Kant and Hegel knew that such drawing or relating *(sich be-ziehen, zeichnen)* implicates an "outside," a "standing outside," an *ecstasis* of sorts. Heidegger's insight is rather different, and it touches not only the three *ecstases* themselves (future, having-been, and present) but also the "mechanism" or "contrivance" or, better, the "event" of ecstatic transport as such. Perhaps the only general hint I can offer for an ecstatic spatiality is this obvious one: whereas traditional views of time and eternity have aligned ecstasy with escape from time and encroachment on eternity in the throes of something other than sex, whether mystical transport or violent sacrificial death, Heidegger takes ecstasy to be the perpetual motion of existence itself. That does not mean that he scorns such throes, but that he takes them to be the throws of time as such. It as though the exceptional temporalities of lovemaking and rapture, the extraordinary times of τίκτειν, those glorious tosses of the dice that are traditionally said to "stop" time in its march, mark the time—and the ecstatic space—of human existence.

What kind of spatiality would correspond to such time and times? What sort of space and spatiality would correspond to the *ecstasis* of the *future*, for example—the projection upon possibilities, in particular the outermost and ownmost possibility of mortality? It would be a space in which every opening or clearing conceals a closure, a mystery, a dark spot or germ, as in a fertilized egg. However, closure is not confinement or containment: the bottom—or, as in Ben Nicholson's Loaf House, the back—always drops out, and the abyss is our sole access to air.

The space of *having-been* would situate us in a tradition that can never be sloughed off but that still has its future ahead of it. No doubt, that future, the future of having-been, may be strange; it may be the future of what Derrida calls "the viewpoint of Oedipus," as Nietzsche and Jean Genet conceive of it. In *Glas*, Derrida cites Genet as follows:

> I understand badly what in art they call an innovator. Should a work be understood by future generations? But why? And what would that signify? That they could use it? For what? I do not see. But I see much better—even though very darkly—that every work of art, if it wishes to attain the most grandiose proportions, must, with an infinite patience and application from the moments of its elaboration, descend the millennia, rejoin, if it can, the immemorial night peopled by the dead, who are going to recognize themselves in this work.

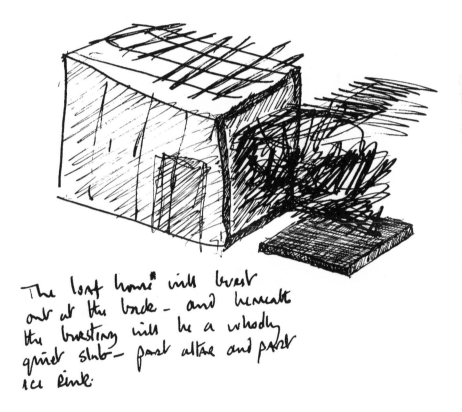

In an already complicated world
the ecstatic cranks up the volume
and suddenly makes it all visible.

The loaf house* will burst
out at the back—and beneath
the bursting will be a wholly
quiet slab—part altar and part
ice rink.

Fig. 10 Ben Nicholson
The Loaf House, 1995
"In an already complicated world the ecstatic cranks up the volume and suddenly makes it all visible. The Loaf House will burst out at the back—and beneath the bursting will be a wholly quiet slab—part altar and part ice rink."

No, no, the work of art is not destined for generations of children. It is offered to the innumerable population of the dead. Who accept it. Or refuse it. But the dead of whom I was speaking have never been alive. Or I forget the fact.[24]

The space of the *present ecstasis* would find itself in falling or slipping, in the *lapsus* and *leakage* where ruination is not merely the future that awaits a work but its irremediable birthmark. For the inception of all projects would transpire in what the early Heidegger calls *Ruinanz,* the "ruinance" of existence. Ruination is the spatiality of the *ecstasis* of the present, and the present presences only as ecstatic ruinance.

As for the ecstatic dynamism of time, rapture or *Entrückung* as such: space would be the very commotion or animation of sudden seizure and release, the periodicity of rapture and rupture, the oxymoron of continuous interruption. It would be the place of displacement and *désœuvrement;* it would be the space of atopia and nomadism; it would be the ultimate uncanniness and "unhomelikeness" of all apparent domesticity—what both Freud and Heidegger call *das Unheimliche,* to which we must now turn. Perhaps the archetictural drawing (or *with*drawing) that would be best suited to ecstatic spatiality would be, not the plan or elevation, but the *section.* A multiplicity of sections, such as Kafka presents in *"Der Bau"* ("The Structure," "The Construction," "The Burrow"), or Rilke in *The Notebooks of Malte Laurids Brigge.*

Ecstatic spatiality would not so much contain or gather as interrupt. It would unfold by way of what Derrida has called the *via rupta,* the effractive or breaching path that can never be charted in advance.[25] Once it is fully liberated, such ecstatic spatiality would stretch to the ends of the world and the earth, embracing not only our deserts of exile, our cities, but also our oases, our sources of

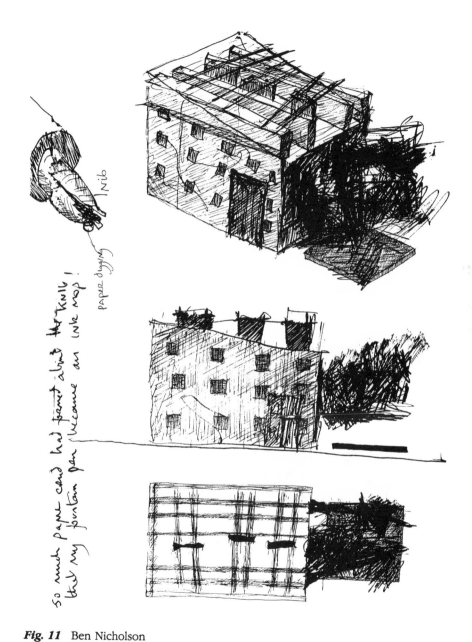

So much paper crud had formed about the knife that my fountain pen became an ink mop!

paper digging

nib

Fig. 11 Ben Nicholson
The Loaf House with paper-digging nib, 1995
"The back will blow out onto slab, and over it. . . . So much paper crud had formed about the nib that my fountain pen became an ink mop!"

respite, all the domains of our being-in or dwelling—even the home that, for all its familiarity, remains utterly uncanny. Ecstatic spatiality, liberated to the greatest possible extent, would no longer be distinguishable from ecstatic temporality—it would be the time-space-play of an always embodied, always uncanny human existence.

III UNHOMELIKE PLACES
Architectural Sections of Heidegger and Freud

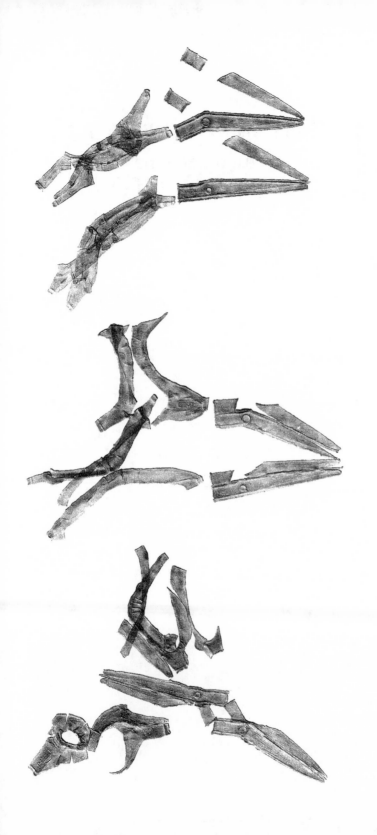

Figs 12–14 Gisela Baurmann
Scissors' Skin (1990–91)
"Quetsch: Investigation into Architectural Representation"
LoPSiA Paris/Briey

Neither a choric space, that is, a space for cosmic lovemaking, nor a liberated ecstatic spatiality can be familiar to us.
Neither has to do with the usual; neither can be reduced
to the technical. Everything about what I am calling *archeticture* is
therefore strange and even uncanny. In the present chapter we
shall call upon Heidegger once again, this time aided and abetted
(or interrupted and frustrated) by Freud, seeking insight into the
unhomelike quality of archeticture. To be sure, we will not dream
of an architectural *plan* or *elevation* composed of equal parts of
Heideggerian ontology and Freudian psychoanalysis. For who
knows what a plan or elevation of Heidegger and Freud would

look like? No one knows. We no longer dream of structures of
thought and knowledge in the way Kant dreamed of them, searching madly for (and failing to find) the bedrock on which to con-
struct a Tribunal of Pure Reason. No, not an elevation of any kind,
nor any plan. Here it can only be an attempt to devise and design
several *archetictural sections,* odd glimpses and cross sections,
snippets of curious alignments and complex configurations in the
bodies of thought of Heidegger and Freud.[1] The thought of each
of the two, taken singly, is of course demanding enough to foil any
amateur archeticton. Such as myself. I shall therefore restrict this
inquiry for the most part to Freud's 1919 essay, *"Das Unheimliche,"*
and Heidegger's 1925 lecture course at Marburg University,
Prolegomena to the History of the Concept of Time.[2] Freud's essay is
contemporaneous with his work on *Beyond the Pleasure Principle,*
his most dazzling speculative work, published in 1920; Heidegger's
lecture course is a kind of first draft of his magnum opus, *Being
and Time,* published in 1927. However, restricting the number of
texts will not really guarantee focus: there is enough material here
for an infinite number of juxtapositions—challenging, thought-provoking juxtapositions. I shall restrain myself, and offer thirty-five
sections.

Heidegger is talking to the editors of *Der Spiegel* in 1966 and looking into the mirror. Ironically, while looking into the mirror, con-
templating his own tarnished political image in the faces of these
journalists, the old man shortchanges himself, cheats his own
thought. He loudly laments the rootlessness and homelessness *(die
Heimatlosigkeit)* of contemporary existence, as though the extirpa-
tion of rootlessness and homelessness had always been the concern of his thought. The contemporary plight is indicated, he says,

by the absence of great art and poetry. It is as though he had never noticed Paul Klee, whose work, however, he cites at the outset of "Time and Being," a piece written only five years before the *Spiegel* interview. (Two decades earlier, Klee's works had been confiscated by the Nazis for the *Entartete Kunstausstellung,* the "degenerate art" exhibition.) It is as though he, Heidegger, were the usual type of neoconservative or reactionary, who turns right in politics when there is nothing left of art. However, for the younger man, for Heidegger the phenomenologist and ontologist, and sometimes even for the mature thinker of mortality, homelessness is nothing to be lamented. It is rather the ontological distinction of humankind, the pristine character of *Dasein* or "existence" as such. Homelessness is what every work of art and archeticture bestows on us: neither roots nor domesticity nor the fireside chat, but a sense of our being never at home in the face of the uncanny.

In *Being and Time* and in the Marburg lecture courses that led up to it, Heidegger defined human existence itself in terms of being *not-at-home.* Indeed, in the first draft of his analysis of care and concern as the fundamental modes of human comportment, Heidegger gathered these existential, ecstatic structures under the larger notion of the unhomelike or uncanny. Section 30 of his 1925 *Prolegomena to the History of the Concept of Time* declares that human existence *(Dasein)* has essentially nothing to do with homey homes, that its very being is *Unheimlichkeit,* "uncanniness," "unhomelikeness." Our being in the world, the world that serves as our only home, is marked by the uncanny discovery that we are *not* at home in it. *Dasein,* or being-there, when it is truly there, is an absentee; it is stamped and typed by the *Unzuhause,* the not-at-home, the nobody-home. Heidegger's thought, early and late, at least until his belated mirror phase, revolves about this paradox or terrible irony: human being is being in the world and dwelling on the earth—and yet we are never at home in the world, never rooted in the earth. When we finally arrive at the "there" of there-being (Da-sein), as Gertrude Stein knew, there isn't any there there. There there is ash—what Freud knew as traces of "the unconscious," and Heidegger as "being toward the end."

Is this feeling of being ill at ease, this uncanny, unhomey sensation—whatever fine distinctions or sweeping claims Heidegger may try to make—merely our fear of death? Or is it more like a pervasive, indeterminate anxiety, a fundamental or founding mood that Heidegger at other times reads variously as joy, melancholy, and, most strikingly, profound boredom? In the face of *what* are we anxious, joyous, melancholy, or deeply bored? Everything and nothing. Everything: beings as a whole. Nothing: no thing at all. An impersonal yet thoroughgoing alienation or expropriation marks our efforts to learn who we are. In his

Indeed, Nathanael's poems were quite boring [sehr langweilig]. His revulsion in the face of Clara's cold and prosaic heart grew more intense; for her part, Clara could not overcome her revulsion in the face of Nathanael's obscure, gloomy, and tedious [langweilige] mysticism. . . . (E. T. A. Hoffmann, The Sandman)

inaugural lecture of 1929, "What Is Metaphysics?" Heidegger finds an appropriately impersonal phrase for it: *Es wird einem unheimlich,* literally, it becomes uncanny for one; more loosely, one begins to feel uncannily not at home, one looks at no one in particular and for no particular reason says, "It's getting strange." Heidegger would insist that this is not an expression of nostalgia, not the predictable homesickness of philosophers, which both Novalis and Nietzsche descried, described, and decried, not anomie, not sentimentality, not the religious longing for a world beyond. And not a mere prologue to the politics of reaction or capitulation to the allures of "leadership."

When and where do human beings begin to feel the uncanniness of human being? Heidegger became increasingly convinced that the *poet's* experience discloses most relentlessly the paradox or terrible irony of human homelessness and disquiet. In the summer of 1927, while discussing Kant—not the most sentimental of thinkers, as we have seen, except perhaps where bedrock is concerned—Heidegger turned to Rainer Maria Rilke's *The Notebooks of Malte Laurids Brigge* in order to get a bit closer to the "fundamental problem" of the manifold meaning of being. Suddenly, instead of an ontology of beings or epistemology of subjects and objects, and instead of Augustine and Aristotle, he invoked the exemplary worlds of the "primitive" and the "child"—Freud's two favorite worlds, the world of totem and taboo and the world of trauma. In order to rejoin these privileged yet remote worlds, as it were, Heidegger injected into his lecture course a piece of poetry, *prose* poetry. About what? About architecture—or perhaps archeticture—in the city. And about ruins. Ruins of home, ruins at home.

The passage from *Malte Laurids Brigge* elaborates a kind of archetictural section, a transversal slice through the middle of a dilapidated apartment building. The slice is produced not on the architect's drawing table, however, but by a wrecker working at the behest of a city planner. Rilke writes:

> Will anyone believe that there are such houses? No, they will say, I'm counterfeiting. This time it is the truth, nothing omitted, and, of course, nothing added. Where would I get it from? You know I'm poor. You know that. Houses? However, to be precise, they were houses that were no longer there.

Houses that had been demolished from top to bottom. What was there were
the other houses, the houses that had stood next to them, high neighboring
houses. Obviously, these were in danger of collapsing, now that everything
next to them had been removed; for a huge framework of long, tarred poles
had been rammed in at an angle between the mud of the vacant lot and the
stripped walls. I do not know whether I've already said that it is these walls
I am referring to. Yet it was not, as it were, the outside wall of the remain-
ing houses (which is what one would have had to suppose) but the inside
wall of the houses that once stood there. One could see the inner surfaces
of these walls. On the various stories one could see the walls of rooms where
the wallpaper still clung, with here and there the hint of a floor or a ceiling.
In addition to the walls of the rooms, a dirty white space ran the entire length
of the brick wall, and through that space crept the open, rust-speckled con-
duits of the toilet pipes, undulating softly in an inexpressibly disgusting
wormlike peristaltic movement. Gray, dusty traces marked the paths that gas
for the lamps had followed along the edges of the ceilings; they twisted all
the way around, here and there, quite unexpectedly, and entered into a hole
in the colored walls, a black gap torn carelessly out of the wall. Most unfor-
gettable, however, were the walls themselves. The resilient life of these
rooms had not let itself be quashed. It was still there; it clung to the remain-
ing nails; it stood on the hand's breadth of floorboard; it had crept under the
hints of corners, where a tiny bit of interior space still remained. One could
see it in the colors that had been transformed ever so slowly over the years:
blue into moldy green, green into gray, and yellow into an ancient and stag-
nant white that was rotting away. Yet it was also in the fresher places that
had been preserved behind mirrors, pictures, and closets; for it had traced
and retraced their contours, and was present in these hidden places too, with
their spiders and dust, places now denuded. It was in every scrap that had
been stripped away, it was in the moist bulges on the lower edges of the
wallpaper, it hovered in the tattered remnants; the repulsive stains that had
come into existence long ago exuded it. And out of these walls at one time
blue, green, and yellow, framed by the fissured paths of the now destroyed
connecting walls, the atmosphere of this life stood out—the resilient, phlegmatic, halting breath that no wind had yet dispersed. There stood the noon-
days and the illnesses, the exhalations and the smoke of years, and the sweat
that pours from armpits and makes our clothes heavy, the fetid breath of
mouths, and the musty smell of fermenting feet. There stood the pungency
of urine, the ardor of soot, the gray steam from boiled potatoes, and the
heavy, slippery stench of fat gone rancid. The sweet and lingering smell of
neglected suckling babes was there, the smell of anxiety in children who go
to school, and the moist heat rising from the beds of growing boys. And
much had joined this company from down below, from the abyss of alley-
ways, everything that had gone up in smoke; and other things had trickled

down from above with the rain, which, above cities, is not pure. And much had been blown in by the weak and domesticated housewinds that always stay in the same street, and much was there from who knows where. I've already said that all the walls had been demolished, all the way back to the rear wall—? Now, this is the wall I've been talking about all this while. You will say that I stood before this wall a long time; but I swear I began to run the moment I recognized it. For that is the terrifying thing—the fact that I did recognize it. Everything I've mentioned here I recognize, and that is why, without the slightest exertion, it runs me through: it is at home in me.[3]

It is at home in me. . . . How strange, how exceedingly strange, to hear Heidegger invoking prose that is not so much purple as moldy green and off-white; uncanny to hear him citing a fiction that extols the resilient life of fetid breath and fermenting feet. There is not another quotation like it in the Heideggerian corpus. Edifying hymns to gods and portentous worries about the destiny of the planet— that is the usual fare with Heidegger. Columns on the march, not cheesy feet; fateful sendings and fatalities of being, not city planning. However, razed walls too are a fatality, the ruins that one recognizes and that run one through. Ruins of home, ruins at home, ruination. Ruinance. I repeat, I do

While conceptualizing buildings as machines eventually led to the demise of meaning in the city of my memory, rational devaluation is violently transcended by this exploded identification. The instruments of torture are also manifestations of architecture as a verb, once and for all replacing the obsolete noun and positing poetic destruction in place of technological building. (Alberto Pérez-Gómez, *Polyphilo,* 1992)

not know another passage in Heidegger as uncanny as this one. And it comes from *Rilke*—the poet he will accuse (in 1942-43) of Schopenhauerianism, botched Christianity, and a kind of sentimental bestiality.[4]

It is at home in me—Rilke. *It* is unhomelike for one—Heidegger. Freud of course has much to say about this *It, Id, Ça,* or *Es.* The

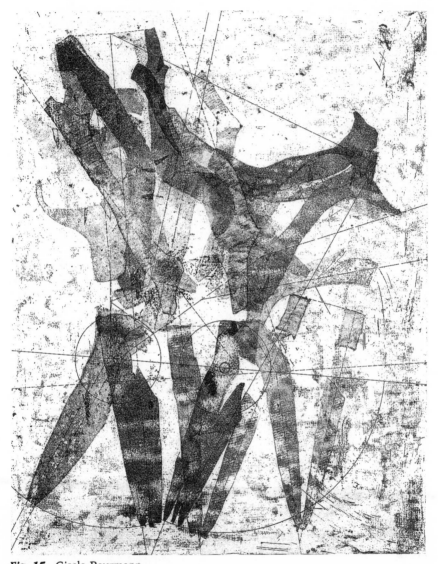

Fig. 15 Gisela Baurmann
Scissors' Skin, etching (1990–91)
"Quetsch: Investigation into Architectural Representation"
LoPSiA Paris/Briey

event that grants time and being, says the later Heidegger; the impersonal life of the drives, the pulsional life that threatens to swallow the diminutive ego, says the later Freud. Both *Es*'s could be read in terms of Maurice Blanchot's neuter/neutral *il*, the narrative voice.

It seemed to me that human faces appeared all around me, but without eyes—instead of eyes, there were profound, horrifying caverns of darkness. "Give me your eyes! Give me your eyes!" cried Coppelius in muffled, moaning tones. (Hoffmann, *S*)

Heidegger never acknowledges the *Es* in Freud. He recognizes it in Rimbaud and Trakl, in the *It gives/There is* of poetry, especially in the "De Profundis" and "Psalm" of Trakl. Yet there is no *Id* in his confrontation with Freudian psychoanalysis: he finds Freud facile and flaccid, a minor character in the history of metaphysical subjectivity. In fact, I know of no serious references in Heidegger (beyond scathing allusions and animadversions) to Freud's oeuvre, not a single positive reference to the *other* great thinker of the uncanny and unhomelike nature of human existence. For his part, Freud, rescued by the time of his *floruit* and by his aversion to philosophy, had less reason to repress *Being and Time* than he did all of Nietzsche, who, as Freud feared, threatened his originality. Freud's allergy to philosophy—philosophy being his first love, that earlier state to which psychoanalysis wends its way via all its detours—and Heidegger's lack of fame (as the *hidden* king) are enough to explain the absence of references in Freud to Heidegger. As for Heidegger's contempt for Freud, *"Das Unheimliche"* may well merit it: it is one of Freud's most tentative, tangential, and inconsequential essays; it is poorly organized, even "lumpy"; it is ostensibly about *aesthetics,* which Heidegger scorns. And yet this essay, uncannily, contains most of Freud's final ideas about psychic life. *"Das Unheimliche"* is about thirty-five pages long, and is divided into three parts. The first part introduces the uncanny or unhomelike as a truant theme of aesthetics or literary criticism; the second provides a quasiphenomenology and a nascent psychoanalysis of the uncanny; the third offers a very odd discussion of the difference between experiencing and reading, *Erleben* and *Lesen*.

The aesthetics of literature, which one usually calls criticism, deals with subdued or sublimated affects, dampened or diluted emotions and feelings, says Freud. One might well wonder why the analyst refers to aesthetics or literary criticism at all, when any patient on the couch reproduces those affects, emotions, and feelings *without* dilution. Perhaps the analyst reads literature for mere diversion. Or perhaps his is a contribution to criticism out of the goodness of his heart and the depth of his experience, an altruism the aesthete could hardly be expected to withstand. Or do literature and its narrative voice here too play a different sort of role? Do they provide access to the not-at-home that no life experience can provide? We will have to return to this question at the end of the chapter—the question of the difference between lived experience and literary gleaning. For the moment, Freud is satisfied to indicate a curious omission in the critical literature: the experience of the uncanny or unhomelike has been neglected, as though it were the (neglected) Heideggerian question of being. What sort of experience is it? One that resists depiction, and one that is hardly uplifting. It is an experience to which Freud himself is scarcely susceptible: he confesses

And with that he seized me so violently that my joints cracked. He unscrewed my hands and feet, reattaching them, first at one place, then another. "They don't fit anywhere else! Better the way they were! The Old Man knew what he was doing!" (Hoffmann, *S*)

or flaunts his obtuseness *(Stumpfheit)* or lack of receptivity with
regard to this subdued emotion. His sober analysis follows two
paths: (1) a quasi-phenomenological description of the uncanny in
life and literature, wherever and however it seems to arise; and (2)
a lexical description of the word as it appears in a battery of dictionaries. It is worth noting that in his presentation of the uncanny
Freud reverses the order of the two paths in his itinerary, present-
ing the dictionary entries first, and only then venturing the description. Both paths, he says, lead to the identical conclusion: the
uncanny is related to terror, anxiety, and horror, and yet perdures
at a safe remove from these affects; the uncanny is thus a species
of the terrifying that points back, not to intellectual insecurity in the
face of some novelty, as Jentsch supposed, but to something long
familiar, something experienced and known of old in a nonintel-
lectual way, something both lost and destined to be found again
in the mists of time. Freud adopts F. W. J. Schelling's definition:
"Un-heimlich is what we call everything that should have remained
secret, in concealment, but that came to the fore." Uncannily, concealment does not wholly conceal; concealment ultimately gives
way to unconcealment; concealment *shows itself* as such. Of all
Freud's essays, this is the one that Heidegger—the thinker of concealing and self-showing—must have read most closely. In secret.
Closely closeted.

By the time Heidegger was teaching his *Prolegomena to the History
of the Concept of Time* in 1925 he would have had four opportunities to read Freud's *"Das Unheimliche,"* which had been published
in four different places. We may be certain that he did not avail
himself of these opportunities. Yet it is worth remembering in some
detail the role that *Unheimlichkeit* plays in Heidegger's budding

ontological analysis of human existence. Uncanniness, or being-not-at-home, is for Heidegger a fundamental structure of existence. Paradoxically, being-not-at-home is to be understood precisely "in terms of being-at-home—familiarity" (*PGZ*, 348). Familiarity is the normal condition or usual state, at least for an existence that is always "falling," always "ruinous," and even "ruinant." If the ruins of home are always at home, always in some sense "familiar," it is because, as we have already heard, human existence is *Ruinanz*.[5] Familiarity itself is a mark of ruinous falling, an expression of evasion. For what is uncanny is the need of existence to *flee from itself*. What is unhomelike is the need of *Dasein* to escape from itself, to be forever fugitive—to be in φυγή, *fuga*, *Flucht*, "flight." To be sure, *die Fuge*, "joining," "jointure," "juncture," appears in Heidegger's texts of the 1930s as an elevating architectonic theme. Nowadays, after the publication of the 1936-38 *Contributions to Philosophy (Of Propriation)*, Heideggerians are waxing lyrical about the "fugal structure" of the maestro's thought. Yet the fugue that is appropriate to Heidegger's thought is on the run somewhere between fear and anxiety. Φυγή is close to πλήγη, a word we shall soon hear in another context; *Flucht*, "flight," is more *Fluch*, "curse" or "plague," than airy fancy. If anxiety is the *ground* of fear, the uncanny is the *abyss* of anxiety. Anxiety *reveals itself* as the fugal structure or flight pattern of an existence ever on the wing: ruinous, ruinant, falling, and—in its very familiarity—fleeing.

Heidegger takes book 2 of Aristotle's *Rhetoric* to be the original text of Western philosophy and psychology on the πάθοι or affects. There the principal πάθος is fear. How to instill fear in the people—perhaps, as Freud reminds us, through the noble lie, which tells of punishments to be meted out in an afterlife, the ruse of Plato's

Republic—or in those who govern. According to Heidegger, Aristotle's analysis, passed on via the Stoa to Augustine, Thomas Aquinas, and the Renaissance and Reformation, remains at the basis of all modern analyses of affectivity. To be sure, Heidegger does not mention Freud. Yet Freud's analysis of anxiety as the affective outcome of *every* repressed emotion, and on the uncanny as the very mark of repression, an analysis that brings the uncanny into closest proximity to anxiety, could certainly be integrated into Heidegger's account of Aristotle's *Rhetoric*. Heidegger's phenomenology of fear and anxiety in 1925 mirrors in an uncanny way Freud's catalog of "lived experiences" in part 2 of *"Das Unheimliche."* This is not the place to rehearse Heidegger's treatment of the *Wovor* and the *Worum*, "that in the face of which" and "that about which" *Dasein* is afraid or anxious. Yet many details of the analysis would fascinate Freud: the "fright" that arises from an immediate, recognized threat, such as a grenade that lands nearby, with only a few seconds before the *Ruck* or tremor of detonation; the "horror" of some unidentifiable threat; the "terror" of sudden horror; the general "anxiousness" of timidity, awe, worry, and so on. Also relevant is Heidegger's insistence on the importance of fear *for* or *about* someone else, the other, whom Freud tends to reduce to the mirror image of a narcissistic projection. However, the purpose of Heidegger's phenomenology of fear is to arrive at that *indeterminate* fear which is generalized anxiety, the anxiety that Heidegger as well as Freud associates with uncanniness. Not only that. Heidegger affirms two of Freud's three principal sites of the uncanny: both thinkers name "darkness" and "solitude" *(Dunkelheit, Alleinsein)* as abodes of the unhomelike, while Freud also writes of "stillness" *(die Stille),* which has a more positive yet also ultimately uncanny resonance for Heidegger. However, not

even these two or three sites are essential to what Heidegger calls
the unhomelike. Rather, *"that in the face of which we are anxious
is the nothing"* (*PGZ*, 401). The no-thing, that is to say, the very dif-
ferential structure of our being in the world, which is never a being
of "things," not even when *Dasein* dies, is what threatens.
Accordingly, that *about* which we are anxious is our being in the
world *as such,* what in *Being and Time* Heidegger calls our *being
able to be* in the world. Our being (able to be) in the world as such
is what is disclosed to us when the *Unzuhause,* our being *not* at
home, comes out of the closet. Heigh-ho, nobody home, as the
child's ditty says: that is what it means to dwell in the world as *possibility-being.* In his 1925 lectures Heidegger calls it our "naked"
being in the world, and he associates the stark nakedness of our
being able to be (not at home) in the world with the abyss and with
mortal anxiety *(der Abgrund, die Todesangst).* The only possible
home for us is the *Un-zuhause, Un-heimlichkeit.* The negative prefix does not simply negate or annul, neither for Heidegger nor for
Freud. Perhaps in memory of Hegel—or of *one* of the Hegels,
namely, the one who thinks the radical exteriority of space and
time—both Freud and Heidegger pursue the monstrously uncanny
power, the positive power, of the negative. Their pursuit should
remind us that however heroic the project of *archeticture* may
sound, elevating tic-talk above τέχνη, there is nothing sentimental
or comforting about that project. Archeticture is as uncanny as
human existence.

According to Freud, the prefix *Un-* is both the mark of repression—
of what criticism has neglected—and a pure supplement to the
word *heimlich,* both necessary and utterly superfluous. For *heimlich* means what is *heim(e)lig, heimisch, vertraut,* which Grimm

calls *vernaculus,* the familiar, homelike, homey. Yet that same word, *heimlich,* also means what is *geheim,* secret, covert, furtive, and hidden, which Grimm calls *occultus,* a word perhaps best rendered by the pseudonegation *(un)heimlich.* It seems clear that *unheimlich* is a species of *heimlich,* not its negation but a positive scion or subset of

She seemed not to notice me, and in general her eyes seemed somehow petrified. I might almost say they were without vision; she appeared to me to be sleeping with open eyes. An altogether uncanny feeling crept over me. . . . (Hoffmann, *S*)

it. Freud will interpret the word's uncanny form as the result of the process of ambivalence: the uncanny will in fact be the most familiar; it will be the skeleton or the flesh in the closet of every home, in the most closely closeted closet of the homiest home there ever was.

Heimlich is a homonym of a special sort. It means both "familiar, domestic, candid" and "unfamiliar, alien, secret." It thus appears to be a primal word, an *Urwort,* of the Abelian sort.[6] Oddly, the contrary and even contradictory meanings of the word induce a kind of reflexivity in Freud's use of it. He twice (*StA,* 4: 248, 250) says that the word *heimlich* "uncannily collapses into its opposite *[mit seinem Gegensatz unheimlich zusammenfällt]."* (The *Standard Edition* sets off the word *unheimlich* in quotation marks on these two occasions, feigning certainty that Freud is merely making *mention* rather than uncanny *use* of the word.) Freud employs the adverb to express, lexically and syntactically, the uncanny conflation of canny and uncanny, homelike and unhomelike, in the same word, as though existence were at home on the wing. His text on the uncanny both constates and performs its subject. Further, the negation of the negative prefix works asymmetrically. That is to say, it affects only the first meaning: *un-heimlich* never means candid,

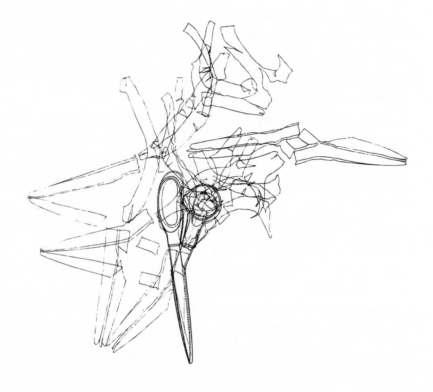

Fig. 16 Gisela Baurmann
Scissors' Skin, drawing overlay (1990–91)
"Quetsch: Investigation into Architectural Representation"
LoPSiA Paris/Briey

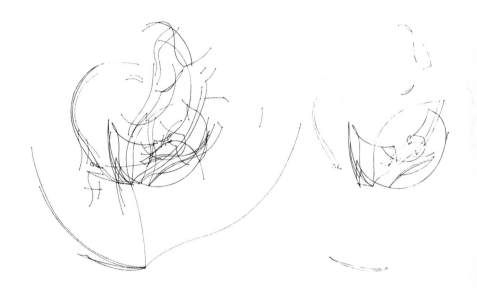

Fig. 17 Gisela Baurmann
Scissors' Skin, drawing abstraction (1990–91)
"Quetsch: Investigation into Architectural Representation"
LoPSiA Paris/Briey

overt, unsecretive. In the second field of meanings, the prefix can only intensify the negative, as though *heimlich* were a Greek word. Heidegger too is intrigued by this word, because he is always on the lookout for the uncanny origins of negation, beyond the workings of propositional and dialectical negation:

> What testifies to the constant and widespread though distorted revelation of the nothing in our existence more compellingly than negation? Yet negation does not conjure the "not" out of itself. . . . For negation cannot claim to be either the sole or the leading nihilative behavior in which Dasein remains shaken by the nihilation of the nothing. Unyielding antagonism and stinging rebuke have a more abysmal source than the measured negation of thought. Galling failure and merciless prohibition require some deeper answer. Bitter privation is more burdensome. (*BW,* 105)

For Freud and Heidegger alike, negation negates the homily of home, the hominy of hearth and haven. No negation of negation leaps out of Hegel's speculative hat in order to rescue dialectic from the monstrous positive power of the negativity that drives it. And yet, in some sense, the negative prefix *does* operate on the unfamiliar, alien, and secret. That is to say, the experience of the uncanny toward which Freud and Heidegger are groping implies the *revelation* of the unfamiliar, alien, and secret. That is the sense of Schelling's insight, which Freud embraces. For it is Schelling's definition of *das Unheimliche,* which Freud sets in spaced type, that successfully relates the two contrary or contradictory senses of the word: if *un-heimlich* designates everything that *ought* to have been kept secret but that now has come to the fore and been revealed, then the word *unheimlich* does in some sense negate the absolutely secretive, the utterly alien, and the wholly unfamiliar. It is as though in the experience of the uncanny and unhomelike, to which the stolid Freud is all but immured, something like *the noth-*

ing—the Heideggerian *Nichts*—announces itself. However subdued the affect, there is in the uncanny a *showing* and a *revealing*. Of what? Of no thing at all.

There is something uncanny about Freud's copying out like Bartleby (or like Bouvard and Pécuchet) those two long dictionary entries on *heimlich,* first from Daniel Sanders, then from the Brothers Grimm, even if it was Theodor Reik who passed the entries along to him. Grimm supplements Sanders (not the Sandman, not just yet) in an odd way. I shall take up the Grimm supplement in a moment. For now, the following uncanny coincidence: as I was working on these dictionary entries in Freud's text, these entries so painstakingly reproduced, so obsessively copied out, as though every lexical detail were of the utmost importance, I received a letter from a German architect, Gisela Baurmann.[7] In her letter, written from Corbusier's *Unité* in Lorraine, Baurmann used words related to *heimlich* four times. I shall present them back to front here, following Freud's example, in order to approach the supplement of the uncanny.

     1. "When I returned from Berlin and Karlsruhe—Berlin was lovely, so familiar *[vertraut],* the streets, the squares, the faces!—I was at first shocked by the bareness and austerity [of Corbusier's *Unité*]. . . . And yet seldom have I felt as unquestionably at home *[ungefragt heimisch]* as I do here." *Heimisch,* not yet unhomelike, not yet uncanny, although introduced by an "And yet." As though one could be at home in the bareness and austerity of Corbusier's abandoned housing for the syndicalist coal miners, in a dwelling that is uncannily betwixt a monument and a ruin.

     2. "For me, all this rigidity (the concrete, glass, corridors, balconies, etc.) has something uncannily *[unheimlich]* calming about it.

Fig. 18 Gisela Baurmann
Scissors' Skin, lead relief (1990–91)
"Quetsch: Investigation into Architectural Representation"
LoPSiA Paris/Briey

Here one feels untouchable. . . . The hardness of all the materials—
the concrete, the dark wood, the unfurnished apartments—radiates
such honesty!" *Unheimlich* is here used adverbially, to modify the
calming effect of the rigid and cold, the tranquilizing effect of glass
and concrete and dark wood, for the sake of an uncanny honesty,
to which I shall also return at the end of the chapter.

3. "Each of us is housed in his or her cell of a cement hon-
eycomb. The edifice itself is a giant, a colossus, planted merciless-
ly in the forest. A tiny, slovenly French village lies ten minutes away
by foot. . . . Yet as soon as you pass through the door [of the *Unité*],
you are taken up and received; as soon as the door closes behind
you, you become part of a tiny secret kingdom, a *heimeligen*
realm." The Swiss, Austrian, and South German *e* now sidles up to
and into the word, in order to suggest an ardor or warmth radiated
(in the *Cité Radieuse?*!) by a hearth or a tile oven, the Allemannic
Kunsht, of which Heidegger was so fond.

4. Finally, Baurmann describes a mechanical iron-ore mine
she inspected somewhere near Briey-en-forêt, a totally automated
work site, altogether unmanned. She writes: "The building was in
disrepair, everything covered by a rust-red dust, and not a soul in
sight. Everything there is automated. It was truly *unheimlich."*
Which is where Freud too begins, without a psyche in sight, and
where he will end, with automata.

In his 1984 introduction to John Hejduk's *The Mask of Medusa,*
Daniel Libeskind refers to "an active trace of homelessness that
remains visible in a cultural atmosphere," adding, "The non-
dwellable establishes itself as a first principle of architecture: a fault
out of which constructive hope emerges, and the destination into
which it collapses when the human promise is broken."[8]

Why does Freud supplement the long quotation from Daniel
Sanders, which gives him the Schellingian definition he will need
for his own idea of repression, with the shorter version from
Grimm? The rather more obscure treatment there, gathered about
the axis *vernaculus/occultus,* gives Freud very little more beyond
what Sanders has already provided, except perhaps for one odd
reference. Grimm cites 1 Sam. 5:12, which recounts Yahweh's
striking the Philistines "in their homelike or secret places *[an heimlichen örten],* so that the city cried to heaven." Freud takes the biblical passage to mean that Yahweh strikes the people—the women
as well as the men, presumably—in their private parts, their
pudenda. That is what this second lexical entry, the Grimm entry,
seems to give Freud. For nowhere in Sanders is there an explicit
reference to the genitalia. However, when one becomes as obsessive as Freud and examines the passage in Samuel, at least in
Luther's translation, something disconcerting happens. Because of
the reference to territory there (*"und alle jre grentze an heimlichen örten"* [1 Sam. 5:6]), and because of the reference to the out-
cry and tumult in the city of the Philistines after some punitive
action by God (*"durch die Hand des HERRN in der Stad ein seer
gros Rumor"* [1 Sam. 5:9]), the *heimlichen örten* at first seem to
imply no more than the local habitations of the Philistines, and
certainly not their private parts. The sense would be that Yahweh
strikes the Philistines in their homes or in their homeland—in
those primary architectural *Umschließungen* discussed by Hegel in
his *Lectures on Aesthetics.* However, a more uncanny sense of
heimlichen örte awaits. A student and friend, Lyat Friedman,
informs me that the Hebrew text says that the hand of Yahweh
struck the Philistines in a *dark place,* cursing them with *hemor-
rhoids.* Thus when the enemies of Israel are blasted by a divine

curse, they suffer from a "homelike plague in homelike places *[und kriegten heimliche Plage an heimlichen örten]*" (ibid.). From the editors of the Luther Bible we learn that while *heim sein* means to be at home, the *heimlich gemach* is the latrine, and a *heimlicher ort* is either a place of ambush (the Greek λόχος), a secret location, or "a veiled expression for the anus or buttocks."[9] *Heimligkeit* means "a secret" in Luther's vocabulary; *heimsuchen* means either to visit or to have intercourse with someone. When God does it, "home-seeking" means either to bless *(Segnen)* or to punish *(Strafen)*, an ambivalence Freud's President Schreber understood better than most contemporary theologians. An uncanny question for the biblical scholar: Is it Yahweh's custom to treat people in the way scapegoats were treated in Greek antiquity—to beat them on their genitals, driving out the demons from the parts that must be made fertile—or to socratize them with blessing and punishment until a painful swelling ensues? Or is Freud's substitution of the private parts for the anal region one of his oddest anal-genito-hermeneutical fantasies? Who here is Oedipus φαρμακός, and who Sphincter?

There is a curious word in Plato's *Phaedrus* (237b 4) describing the crafty lover of youths, the canny lover who cunningly convinces boys that he is in fact *not* a lover, so that they ingenuously place all their trust in him. The word is αἱμύλος. Ficino translates it as *vir sane versutus,* a man well versed in the ways of the world (*versutus,* from *verto,* I turn). One thinks of Odysseus πολύτροπος. Aeschylus has Prometheus tell of his "counsels of craft" on behalf of the Olympian gods, after the Titans had scorned his "clever machinations," αἱμύλας μηχανὰς (*Prometheus Bound,* line 208). Αἱμύλος sounds very much like *heimlich,* uncannily so, especially in its homeliest of down-home forms, the South German *heimelig*. To be sure, no self-respecting philologist would venture an etymology beyond the Nordic *Heim* for the whole sequence of German words; there is certainly no need to hearken back to some Greek etymon, one that would displace the "home" from the German *heimlich*, as though *heimlich* were a Greek word, intensified as *un-heimlich*. Yet it is tempting to think that the wheedling and wily lover, the seducer whose speeches are also often described as δεινόν, clever, sly, cunning, canny, uncannily foxy, is himself the creature that is normally kept in the closet. Or beaten about the genitals.

According to the second part of Freud's *"Das Unheimliche,"* there are two main sources of the unhomelike and uncanny in life and in letters: (1) the return of materials and complexes repressed during infancy, and (2) the reemergence of atavistic beliefs and superstitions that humanity has (if only in intellectual terms) already overcome. These two sources follow the familiar ontogeny-phylogeny parallel in Freud, homologous with the psychophysical parallelism, with each human infant serving as the microcosm that in some way mirrors the macrocosm of humankind's infancy. In both cases (for Freud's examples seem to cross all the parallels), both infantile humanity and human infancy come into question. Both sites involve the no-man's land that divides the living and the dead, a realm peopled by puppets and automata. Freud's famous reading (or misreading) of E. T. A. Hoffmann's *Der Sandmann* occurs here, although I will say little about it. (To insist on Freud's *misreading* seems jejune to me: while Freud distorts certain details of Hoffmann's story, his reading remains an astonishing and even uncanny achievement.) One might try to trace the same obses-

sions—the automaton that both thrills and kills, the beautiful puppet that both seduces to life and induces death—in Melville's "The
Bell-Tower," Mérimée's "La Vénus d'Ille," Poe's "Ligeia" and
"William Wilson," and Mary Shelley's *Frankenstein*. What fascinates
Freud in Hoffmann's tale are two duplex and duplicitous figures:
the sandman, here called Coppelius and Coppola, who burns and
plucks out the eyes of children, and Olimpia, the enucleated puppet who tears out the hearts of young men. For Freud, the character called Nathanael—the boy who is terri-
fied by the sandman (embodied in the   Clara can by no means be
                                        said to have been beautiful;
threats of his governess) and the youth who   that is what everyone
is so enamored of Olimpia that he scorns the   agreed whose office it was
                                        to know about beauty. Yet
love of his faithful Clara—is reminiscent of   the architects praised the
the Wolfman, who adopts a feminine posi-   flawless proportions of her
                                        figure.... (Hoffmann, S)
tion vis-à-vis the father. Again, both cases,
both sources of the unhomelike in life and letters, apply to the second of the two motifs in the sandman story—the doppelgänger, the
doubling and redoubling marked, to repeat, by the names
Coppelius-Coppola (from the Italian *coppo,* "eye socket") in
Hoffmann's tale. Freud sees in the doppelgänger the original *Di
Manes,* the guardian spirits or tutelary genii, the good daimons that
now, under the new religion, under the aegis of new paternal pow-
ers, become demons. Among the more familiar doppelgänger are
the feet, the left and the right, of an erect humanity. The feet,
whose odor offends the obsessively visual human being, the creature that can no longer stand to see its feet, much less suffer their
fermentation. What is least homelike and most uncanny is that
which is always at home: the human body in all its anonymity and
imperious power, with all its gravity and in all its levity, in and out
of all the holes and empty ciphers of its desires—the original dou-

ble, which the wind blew in from who knows where, Descartes
certainly cannot figure it out, while Heidegger can only say that it—
the body—is "the most difficult problem."[10] For the double, left
and right, female and male, has no origin, and marks the end of all
originary thinking. Freud's lumpy essay limps along from here to
Nietzsche's thought of eternal recurrence of the same, and from
thence to repetition compulsion, the economy of lifedeath, and primary masochism—all the atavisms that psychoanalysis would have
preferred to let lie but that make psychoanalysis psychoanalysis.
Which, Freud says, many take to be *unheimlich*.[11]

Repression is the very mechanism of anxiety, according to Freud;
any affect or emotion that is repressed returns as anxiety. Further,
its return is uncanny—the emergence of something both long
familiar and long hidden that ought to have remained in concealment. Heidegger speaks of the concealment and even distortion of
beings that are always a part of their epiphany. Yet it may be that
Heidegger's thought of self-concealing being as enigma, mystery,
and secret *needs* the thought of repression. For when repression is
primal, when it is *Ur-Verdrängung*, it is utterly beyond all thought
of beings. Repression, for its part, has to be thought in terms of the
ontological difference. The uncanny, unhomelike return of the
repressed is a thought *of being*, subjective genitive, precisely
because in it there is no subject.

Rudolf Arnheim, to whom we referred in the preceding chapter,
cites a second and a third example of architectonic thought after
Kant (*DAF*, 273). After he mentions Marcel Proust's own depiction
of *À la recherche du temps perdu* as a medieval cathedral, with
each part of the work designed as a porch or a stained-glass win-

dow in the apse, he cites Freud's *New Series of Lectures toward an Introduction to Psychoanalysis* (1932-33). He reproduces Freud's "modest drawing" of the second topological system, reminiscent of, but different from, his more famous drawing in *The Ego and the Id* (1923).

"Can you not see me? Coppelius deceived you: those were not my eyes that burned their way into your breast; they were ardent drops of your own heart's blood—I still have my eyes, look at me!" (Hoffmann, *S*)

Arnheim comments as follows:

> Freud undertakes to describe the complex interrelation between two sets of fundamental psychoanalytic concepts, namely unconscious, preconscious, and conscious [the *first* topical or topological system, usually called the *dynamic* system, understandably of enormous importance to the author of *The Dynamics of Architectural Form*], and id, ego, and superego [the *second* topical or topological system]. The principal dimension to be represented is that of the distance from the station point of consciousness, i.e., the dimension of depth. Hence an elevation is more appropriate than a horizontal plan. (*DAF*, 273-74)

For Arnheim, consciousness is "the station point." The unconscious, which is deep, lies at a remote distance from the station. Arnheim neglects to mention that in all editions of Freud's works prior to the *Standard Edition,* Freud's "modest sketch," ostensibly appropriate only in elevation, was shown *on the horizontal*—probably in order to save space, say the editors of the *Standard Edition* and the *Studienausgabe* (*StA,* 1: 515 n. 1). No doubt, such a horizon(t)al positioning of Freud's sketch further enhances its appearance as an eye—a bit squashed, to be sure, and therefore reminiscent of the eye of J. D. Salinger's "Laughing Man." What lends credence to its *being* an eye is perhaps the fact that—in the German, at least— consciousness is always defined as the system W-Bw, *Wahrnehmung-Bewußtsein,* roughly, perceptual consciousness, or perception-plus-consciousness.

Never in his life had he come across an optical instrument that brought objects right up to the eye so purely, so sharply, in such clear outlines. (Hoffmann, *S*)

Arnheim notes Freud's own complaint that his drawing is not true to scale: the region of the id or unconscious would have to be significantly larger than those of the ego or the preconscious and perceptual-conscious. "This flaw, however," Arnheim adds, "is of minor importance, because the drawing is topological rather than metric" (*DAF,* 274). Moreover, the use of curved lines indicates that these are only approximate—suggested and suggestive—spaces. Arnheim stresses that Freud's drawing is "entirely visual," and goes on to suggest that "if it were to be executed as a building, the

"Do me a favor, brother," said Siegmund to him one day. "Do me a favor and tell me how a clever fellow like you could go ogling that wax doll over there, that wooden puppet?" (Hoffmann, *S*)

working-out of the actual shapes and dimensions could continue from here without a break" (ibid.). The oddity, the truly uncanny nature of the drawing— the fact that Freud represents unrepresentable psychic forces to a *perceptual consciousness* that is itself represented in (or immediately above) the drawing, indeed, represented as a relatively insignificant supplement to the system, a mere superficies, a kind of lens or cornea or cap—Arnheim does not mention. He takes the fact that Freud *has* to draw drawings for a perceptual consciousness to be the visualist's victory. What Arnheim neglects to ask is: How much of the building would be built by the id, presuming that the powerful id can read drawings? And if only the ego can read and build, what will it make of the id at its foundations? Finally, if we compare this drawing to Freud's earlier sketch of the second topological system in *The Ego and the Id,* one uncanny addition strikes us:

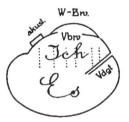

The figure of Olimpia hovered before him in the gentle winds, emerged from the bushes, and gazed at him from the radiant brook with magnificent, beaming eyes. (Hoffmann, *S*)

The eye is now oddly squashed or sunken, no longer almond in shape, but sacklike, collapsing under its own weight—or under the weight of the new addition. Above the protuberance of the id or *Es* on the left is an "acoustical cap," *Hörkappe,* presumably the "Wernicke speech center" in the brain, which plays a role in the hearing/understanding of language. Freud compares the entire W-Bw system, the perceptual conscious, to the fertilization spot *(Keimscheibe)* that sits on top of an egg. (Luckily, the superego has not yet arrived on the scene at this stage of Freud's account, so that such a simile remains possible.) From the very beginning of his career, Freud placed great importance on speech and hearing in his accounts of the preconscious and the functioning ego. Clearly, were one to *build* Freud's psychic system, one would need more than a visualist architect. When Arnheim speaks of Freud's drawing as "actually the translation of a system of forces into a perceptually tangible medium," with the metaphor or kinesthesia of "tangibility" left undefined, and when he cites the superego as the "opening" or "bridge" from the id to the ego or "liberating realm of consciousness," deftly surmounting the "horizontal barrier that blocks this upward motion," one wonders how much Freud our architect has understood. Presumably, all that Freud ever wanted to understand and build was the solid double line of *repression*, on a tangent to the dotted double line between id and ego, or, on the right side of the sack system, the double line that seems more like a canal to the outside world than a bar-

An angry Nathanael sprang to his feet, repulsing Clara from him: "Damn you, you lifeless thing, you robot!" (Hoffmann, *S*)

rier. What *is* the double line of *Verdrängung?* That is Freud's question to the psychoanalytic architect who has done this drawing. Is it a trapdoor? open door? diving board? pendulum? And what *is* the repressed itself, which, in spite of all its drawn appearances, itself never appears—except perhaps to return *as* repressed in the phenomenon of the uncanny? No architect, but only an archetict, could pursue these questions.

The automaton or puppet—Descartes's man in the street or Kleist's boxing bear and ballet dancer in *Das Marionettentheater*—is the uncanny other, the doppelgänger. It is never far from home. Even when she or he is of the opposite gender, as the enucleated Olimpia, it is "the voice of the friend that every *Dasein* carries with itself."[12] The mute automaton arrogates to itself the daimonic voice of conscience and the demonic voice of guilt. The origin of the

doppelgänger, both in the narcissism of the
individual psyche and in the tutelary genius or
daimon of a culture, would contain the secret

"Only in Olimpia's love
will I find my Self again."
(Hoffmann, *S*)

of primal repression. It would be the ultimate source of anxiety and
of anxiety's shade, the uncanny. It would be the origin of auto-
affection, of hearing and understanding oneself while speaking;
hence, the origin of all reflexivity and consciousness, the origin of
all oneiric presence in metaphysics. Such "origins" can only be
nonorigins: the doppelgänger always comes first.

Olimpia, the alluring but dangerous puppet—a kind of Edwina
Scissorhands—built by Schelling's and Hegel's favorite scientist,
Spalanzani, and given Nathanael's eyes by Coppola-Coppelius, is a
technitron. Nathanael first sees her through Coppola's pixelated
Perspektiv or technological looking glass. Indeed, he *always* sees
her through the doppelgänger's looking glass, so that Nathanael
seems to be the technitron of his own envisaging, the architect or
Demiurge of his own disaster. Hoffmann teases his readers from the
very start of the tale, where we are told that the sandman desires
"to observe quite closely the mechanism of [Nathanael's] hands and
feet," so that Coppelius in fact proceeds to "unscrew" the boy's
appendages, reattaching them here and there, until he is forced to
admit defeat.[13] As a young suitor, Nathanael inveighs against his
fiancée Clara for failing to respond ardently enough to his gloomy
poetry. He accuses her of being an automaton (*S*, 25), thus betray-
ing the fact that *every* woman he looks at appears to him (in his
perspective, which is the doppelgänger's *Perspektiv*) to be the man-
nequin that *he* is. In a word, if Olimpia's seductive gaze *(Anblick)*
communicates love to Nathanael, that gaze is Nathanael's own look
(An-blick) directed at her gaze. Hers are the "magnificent, beaming

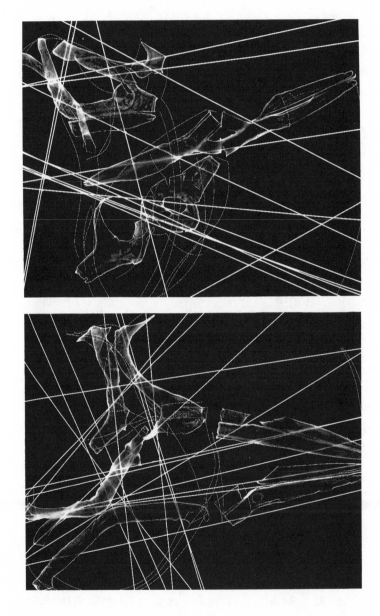

Figs. 19, 20 Gisela Baurmann
Scissors' Skin, rayograms (1990–91)
"Quetsch: Investigation into Architectural Representation"
LoPSiA Paris/Briey

eyes" that look back at him "from the radiant brook" *(aus dem hellen Bach)* of his own narcissism (*S,* 30). Freud's worst nightmare: the ultimate victory of a narcissism so primary that there is no escaping its deadly doubling effects. "Well may Olimpia seem *unheimlich* to you cold, prosaic human beings," cries Nathanael. "Her loving gaze rose like the sun *for me alone,* permeating my senses and my thoughts . . ." (*S,* 35). Everywhere he looks, Nathanael sees Olimpia's imperious gaze, or Clara's Olimpian gaze, upon him; it is the gaze that will incite him to plunge to his own death. Heidegger's worst nightmare: the essence of technology is a mode of disclosure so overwhelmingly powerful that it blinds us to all other modes, cutting them off as possibilities for us. Heidegger's dearest hope: the disclosure enacted in and by the work of art, especially the work of poetry, the work of language, will resuscitate the disclosure of disclosure as such. Yet what about a poetry or fiction (such as E. T. A. Hoffmann's) whose technique (in the Greek sense of poietic art) confounds nature and artifice, producing a truly ticno-techno-phantasm? What about a work of art that puts to work the art of the technical artificer and the tictonic lover-deceiver? This would be betrayal from below, from the South. For they are all Italians, these Futurist ticnotechnowizards: Spalanzani, Coppola, Rappaccini, Bannadonna (the last two from Hawthorne's "Rappaccini's Daughter" and Melville's "The Bell-Tower," respectively), joined by Casanova and his doll. One recalls Freud wandering anxiously through the red-light district of a small Italian town, uncannily unable to flee, returning again and again to the street where he first recognized the significance of the neighborhood, confronting again and again a fate worse than death. Luckily, Heidegger brought Frau Heidegger along, to help him find his way unscathed through Rome.

The sandman burns and extracts the eyes of naughty children who disobey their mothers and will not go to bed. Such is Derrida's anxiety in *Mémoires d'aveugle*.[14] Such is the academicians' anxiety in the face of Derrida. Which is why they try to scratch out his eyes.

Hoffmann calls Coppola the "accursed *Doppeltgänger [sic] und Revenant.*" Derrida begins a recent book on Heidegger, *Of Spirit*, by invoking the *revenant,* the ghost, the return of the repressed.[15] Spiriting Heidegger in the direction of *Geist,* Derrida reveals the uncanniness of Heidegger's corpus and his politics. Which is why Heideggerians in particular try to scratch out Derrida's eyes.

Heidegger's most stubborn doppelgänger in *Being and Time* is none other than the concept of the "self." He continues to appeal to it (as Narcissus to the stream) even after the ecstatic analysis of temporality has left it in tatters. He fails to recognize that all appeals to the self *(das Selbst)* and to propriety *(Eigentlichkeit)* are haunted by the Augustinian-Cartesian ghost—the *cogito.* Freud cites the thought of eternal recurrence of the same in the context of the endless splitting or fission of the father-imago *and* of the ego. That would be eternal return as Pierre Klossowski thinks it in *Le cercle vicieux,* with the "self" enucleated and catapulted from itself, with all our selves on the endless cycle of anamnesis and amnesia.[16]

Recall Heidegger's and Augustine's anxiety in the face of *concupiscentia oculorum,* and Augustine's desire to be castrated for the sake of the kingdom of heaven—his need to adopt a feminine position before the divine father. That would be the anxiety, not of losing one's eyes, but of keeping them: an overwhelming horror in the face of the temptations of visibility, Olimpia's seductive

Anblick, the rayogram of her gaze, her vision, her sight, which is the very sight of her—for, again, her eyes are Nathanael's own eyes—in the *Perspektiv* of the doppelgänger. Bannadonna, says Melville. Narcissus, says Freud; *abscisus,* says Augustine. Oh, to be spayed (the Latin *spado*) for the sake of the father. Desire for the Great Dark of the solar anus. Olimpia's bloody eyes, enucleated by Coppola, are Nathanael's *seeing* eyes—glued to the *Perspektiv.* Heidegger's love of clearing is surpassed by his love of concealing, the mystery, *das Geheimnis,* where the *Heim* of *Geheim* is always *un-heimlich.* This puts him too close to Freud for comfort.

And how could we fail to refer back to the sexual act, and especially to the feminine sex as place? In its likely confusion with the first "house" of man, but also its confusion with his *skin?* In some way, the feminine sex ought to serve as a skin for the man's sex, for the man himself, who is without access to this other dimension: the mucous. Dimension of the sexual act? Of its accessibility, its economy, its communion beyond skins. (Irigaray, *E,* 50)

The mother's body too is a site of the uncanny unhomelike. It is the occasion of fantasies of life-in-the-womb, to be sure: the fascination exercised by intrauterine existence—as Descartes discusses it in his 1648 correspondence with Arnauld. Descartes says that the infant, who will retain no recollection of its life in the mother's womb, must nonetheless *constantly* be cogitating, gathering, and thinking *itself* as existing, even as the animal spirits of *her* blood course through its arteries and nerve tubes. No wonder weaning is such a thought-provoking experience. At the same time, according to Freud, the female genitalia represent the uncanny unhomelike—at least for "neurotic males"—so that the site and sight of

She gives form to the man's sex, and sculpts it from the inside. She becomes the containing one, and the active *place* of the sexual act. . . . Is she not imagined to be passive only because the man fears the loss of mastery in the act? Whence his violence from time to time? (Irigaray, *E,* 49)

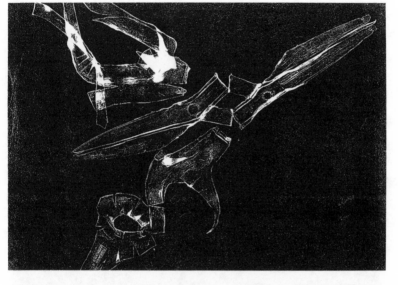

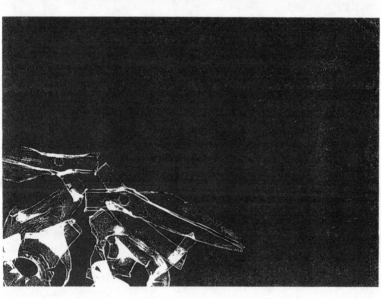

Figs. 21, 22 Gisela Baurmann
Scissors' Skin, rayograms (1990–91)
"Quetsch: Investigation into Architectural Representation"
LoPSiA Paris/Briey

love inspire both homesickness and horror, being both Dido's cave and the head of Medusa.

Would it be possible to think together the enucleated eye or weeping mucous mouth of the male member and the lips of woman? Not for the sake of the witch's brew and warlock's stew of phallic mother or vaginal father, but for the sake of difference without war? Without war or even litigation, the contemporary way to make love? Would it be possible to think the mouth and lips together as enveloping envelopes?

> In love, it would be fitting for the parts of the whole—the union of man and woman—to envelop one another *mutually*, rather than for each to destroy the envelope of the other. (Irigaray, *E*, 58)

What Freud calls the *Kinderangst* of losing one's eyes is actually the projection of a parental, paternal/maternal anxiety, the terror of every adult who watches the infant child wielding its first pair of scissors, fumbling about the face and eyes. *Kastrationsangst* shared by mother and father, both in terror of losing the child's eyes. Testimony to the love that Freud sees disturbed by Coppelius, the child's love for its slain father. The child's anxiety is twofold: first, that the violent father will throw sand in its eyes, will continue to say *no* in the name of the father; second, that the gentle father will die, never knowing of the child's *yes* to him. The child's embrace of the father, the sometimes violent, sometimes gentle father, is perhaps both a concession to the unquenchable hatred and a plea for recognition of the ardent love. Aristotle and Hegel say that it is perfectly obvious that parents love their children more than their children love them. Not so. Not more. Perhaps not even differently. Children fear for their fumbling parents as well. "It's okay, Papi, it's just your nerves." Nietzsche says somewhere that fathers are always a bit awkward, even after they have become ghosts.

The eye dislodged from the socket (coppo) in the head and in the male member: a century before Bataille, whose phantasm of the pineal eye we will meet in the fourth and final chapter, Novalis saw the doppelgänger in this unseeing eye and spewing mouth. If Heidegger, the thinker of the clearing and of ocular concupiscence, ever saw it, he never said so. Because the thought of being and propriation soars beyond the whole of beings, it misses, as Sartre averred, the holes in beings. Yet nothing, the no-thing of the granting, is all Heidegger ever desired. Hence the scathing polemics against psychoanalysis. Hence the naïveté of a lordly Heidegger dispensing wisdom to the analysts at Zollikon.[17]

If the doppelgänger is originally the daimon, tutelary genius, or soul—as guarantor of immortality—she or he or it soon becomes the herald of death, as in Kenneth Branagh's Dead Again. This is the historical unhomelikeness of anxiety, which Freud finds in Heine's late work, Die Götter im Exil. Heidegger needs this thought, and this poet, for his encounter with Hölderlin, the thinker of the mortality of all gods; he needs Heine as well as Nietzsche for his thought of "the last God," who passes by "the futural ones."[18]

There is something particularly uncanny about the third and final part of Freud's "Das Unheimliche." Freud would very much like to distinguish between "lived experience" and "reading," life and letters. Heidegger triumphant: without really knowing the Freudian text, he predicted all along that Freud was mired in Erlebnis, the mush of "lived experience" that life-philosophy dishes out in order to prove to itself that it is not moribund. According to Heidegger, "lived experience" is the very death of thought, the funeral mask of metaphysics. What is uncanny about Freud's effort is that *all* his sources for the uncanny are literary; even what he claims to be auto-biographical "lived" experiences are of course marvelously narrated and beautifully crafted pieces of writing—no matter how lumpy the essay as a whole. Freud triumphant: without ever knowing the Heideggerian text, Freud sensed the inevitable turn to poetry—and even to literature—demanded of all thinking.

In the fairy tale, writes Freud, virtually everything *is* uncanny, so that nothing is experienced *as* uncanny. It is as though the willing suspension of disbelief both conjures and quiets the uncanny, both spurs and neutralizes the unhomelike at once. Freud has to settle for the paradox "that in literature *[Dichtung]* much is not *unheimlich* that would be *unheimlich* if it occurred in real life, and that likewise in literature possibilities abound for attaining *unheimlich* effects that do not occur in real life" (*StA*, 4: 271-72). Life and letters engage in a kind of ring dance of canny/uncanny indetermi-nacy. However, the amulet of literature serves less well against the ghosts of repressed materials from infancy—materials long familiar to us yet heretofore locked away in the unconscious, *altvertrautes Verdrängtes*—than it does against the collective atavisms of early humanity. The uncanny unhomelike thus returns to each life, even to the most stolidly unphilosophical and immured of existences, in the life of letters.

It is unhomelike with one; it is at home in me.

Freud refers in particular to three anxieties of childhood, anxieties that never fail to produce uncanny and unhomelike effects and affects in both life and letters:

Stillness

"The resilient, phlegmatic, halting breath that no wind had yet dispersed . . ."

". . . seldom have I felt so unquestionably at home."

Solitude

"The smell of anxiety in children who go to school . . ."

". . . here one feels untouchable."

Darkness

"A black gap torn carelessly out of the wall . . ."

". . . radiates such honesty!"

Fig. 23 Gisela Baurmann
Scissors' Skin, drawing overlay (1990–91)
"Quetsch: Investigation into Architectural Representation"
LoPSiA Paris/Briey

IV UNHOMELIKE BODIES

Corporeal Space in Merleau-
Ponty, Bataille, and Irigaray

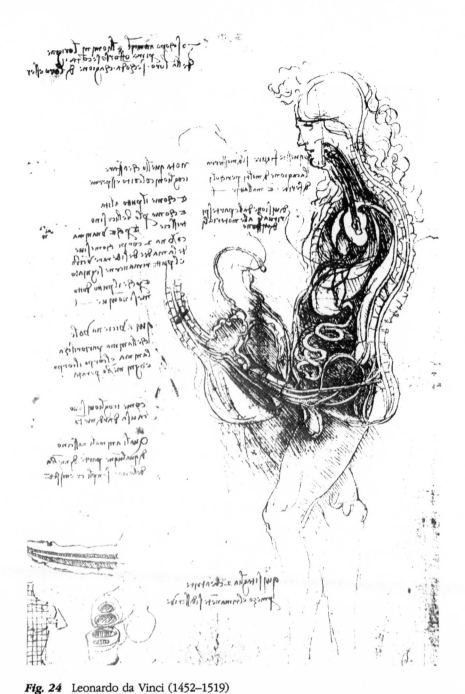

Fig. 24 Leonardo da Vinci (1452–1519)
Genito-urinary system (detail), ca. 1500
"I display to men the origin of their second—first or perhaps second—cause of existence."[1]

The ebbs and flows, weights, rhythms, and surges that emanate
from us are inherent in the body and its movements.
—Robert J. Yudell

Human bodies are not opaque material masses whose axis of
position and diagram of movement we scan and interpret.
They move in the environment engendering profiles and tele-
scoping images of themselves, casting shadows, sending off
rustlings and echoes.
—Alphonso Lingis

Allow me to return to the outset of this book—and also to the outset of a long tradition in cosmology and anthropology. A Pythagorean astronomer and mathematician, Timaeus of Locri, visits Athens on a festival day of Pallas Athena. He promises to regale the goddess (and Socrates) with a discourse on the creation of the body and the soul of the universe and of humankind. His start-ing point seems perfectly obvious to him, and it also seems to have convinced philosophers, critics, and architects from Philo through Hegel, Palladio through Arnheim. Timaeus divides *everything*, every-thing in the universe, into two. That is to say, he divides *something* into two—it is hard to say *what* he divides, inasmuch as the universe

Division of woman into two: often devalorized in her relation to the fluid, valorized in her relation to the solid. Yet this valorization is ambiguous in what most concerns her, depriving her as it does of her greatest subtlety: place as such, the place she contains, invisibly. (Irigaray, *E*, 57)

of being is only one side of his division. On the one hand, clearly the more elevated hand, Timaeus envisages *perdurant being*, which is invisible to the eye and inaccessible to every human faculty except pure thought. On the other hand, the more lowly hand, Timaeus touches upon *mutable becoming* or γένεσις, which is visible and accessible to all the senses but intractable to thought.

Timaeus's two hands generate an enormous paradox, which we hinted at in chapter 1. The Demiurge and father, craftsman and progenitor, technician and sire of genesis produces or begets becoming by "looking up" to invisible being. He models visible becoming on invisible being. He takes what-is as his paradigm, and by some miracle of ineptitude produces or reproduces a copy or imitation of it, a μίμημα of pure being, which is said to be becoming or genesis, genesis itself being a mixture of what-is with what-is-not. Thus the result of his modeling or mating, however splendid (and Timaeus wants to honor the goddess and Socrates by singing its praises), is held to be inferior to the being on which it is modeled. Yet how can such slippage from the superior to the inferior *be*, or even *come* to be?

Obviously, both the modeling and the fathering relations require a *third kind*, somewhere between what-is and what-is-not,

Khôra does not form a couple with the father, in other words, with the paradigmatic model. Third in kind (48e), she does not pertain to an oppositional pair, for example, that which

"within which," as it were, being and nonbeing can mix and match, mate—and deteriorate. Timaeus searches for that third kind somewhere between high and low, paradigm and (botched) icon, original ánd (poor) copy, a kind that is invisible and yet not truly accessible to pure thought. As we heard in chapter 1, this third genus can be approached only by way of λογισμῷ τινι νόθῳ , a "bastard" or "illegitimate" calculation or account. Marsilio Ficino translates this phrase as *adulterina quadam ratione,* "a reason that is to some degree adulterated," or "to some degree a bastard reason." Schelling translates the phrase that means to describe our difficult approach to the third kind as *durch falsche Imagination,* "by means of the false imagination." Hieronymus Müller translates it ingeniously (or ingenuously) as *durch ein gewisses Afterdenken,* "by means of a certain *posterior* thinking," taking the word *After* in both its senses— as the *subsequent* and as the *anal region,* the Philistine "behind," suitably socratized by the Lord. The third kind, hovering between being and becoming, can be approached only in secret places, *an heimlichen örten,* by means of a kind of posterior analytics.[2]

The third kind, "in which" or even "out of which" becoming is to be modeled or engendered and nurtured, is itself amenable to neither sensibility nor thought. It is somehow neutral, because it must "receive all things" without distorting them. Timaeus says, as we have heard, that it must be "like the base of a perfume," an odorless pomade that can be permeated by any and every fragrance. It must be

the intelligible paradigm forms with sensible becoming, which more closely resembles the couple father-son. The "mother" would be apart. And because this is only a figure or scheme, thus one of the determinations that *khôra* receives, *khôra* is *no more* a mother than she is a nurse, and no more a nurse than she is a woman. This *triton genos* is not a *genos,* first of all because it is a unique individual. It does not belong to the race of women *(genos gynaikôn).* *Khôra* marks a place apart, the spacing that preserves a rapport of dissymmetry with everything that, "in her," at her place, or beside her, seems to form a couple with her. In the couple outside the couple, we can no longer consider this strange mother, the mother that grants place without engendering, to be an origin. She escapes every anthropo-theological scheme, escapes all history, all revelation, all truth. Preoriginary, *prior to* and outside all generation, she no longer even has the meaning of a past time, of a present that has passed. *Prior to* does not signify any temporal anteriority. The relation of independence, the nonrapport, more closely resembles that of the interval, or of spacing, when it comes to what lodges there, in order to be received there. (Derrida, *K*, 92) like a slab of pure wax, or a mixing bowl, or a hollow hiding somewhere in the interstices of being and becoming. This shapeless slab, crater, hollow, or harbor Timaeus calls χώρα.[3] Χώρα eventually becomes the Latin *regio, locus,* and *spatium,* the "space" that will be articulated by all architectures and occupied by all Western human bodies hence.

However, the architectures prove to be uncanny, and the bodies in the spaces of architecture prove to be unhomelike bodies, even before we spell the word new. Χώρα, which we can approach only by way of an illegitimate or bastard discourse, is said to be the "nurse of becoming," the "mother" or "womb" of the universe. She is not only the space and stuff of all becoming but also, according to Timaeus, the consort of the father; she is not only the workshop of the craftsman but also his helpmate. Whoever she is, she opens the space of all paradox and oneiric speculation. For even though she is said to be neutral (from *ne/uter,* "neither/nor"), neither being nor becoming, neither thinkable nor sensible, neither elevated nor lowly, χώρα must somehow be *both,* and even *more than both.* She must somehow be *otherwise.* For if she may not be a she, she most certainly is not a he. She must somehow be the source of both the Demiurge's successful modeling-and-fathering and all slippage-and-retrogression from the lofty to the base. However, Timaeus remembers only the lapse and the ruination, not the encompassing and the giving: at the end of a discourse that is supposed to honor the goddess Athena and the philosopher-midwife Socrates, Timaeus declares womankind and "all things female" to be barely one degree above the brute. He also concedes, at the very end, that astronomers (and all technowizards?) are sometimes birdbrains.

If Timaeus's account of the craftsman soon leaves the *father*

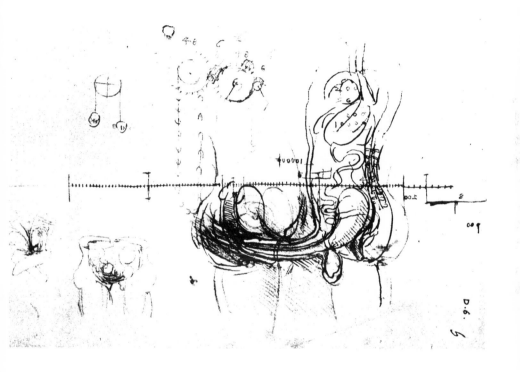

Fig. 25 Leonardo da Vinci (1452–1519)
Coition figures in sagittal section, ca. 1493–94
Note the mechanical drawings at the shoulders of the female figure—pulleys, chains, buckets, counterweights, all traditionally employed in raising water, dredging, and so on—an odd combination of the hydraulic and the mucous.

behind, and never goes to meet the *mother* or nurse of a generated and living universe, how far have we come since his time? Are there any recent signs of a return to the neglected genesis of genesis? The present inquiry into *archeticture* will conclude by referring to three such signs.

Merleau-Ponty and the Flesh of the World

Galileo and Descartes are doubtless two of Timaeus's distant descendents. It is their objective, homogeneous, geometric space (criticized by Heidegger in chapter 2 and further discussed with reference to Husserl in the appendix, below) that Maurice Merleau-Ponty tries to displace by means of his analyses of the spatiality of the lived body—of the body proper, my own body, for me and for others. Merleau-Ponty's body is not the Cartesian fresh cadaver, with its pliable springs and levers infinitely stilled, putatively ready for ensoulment by an outside agent but fundamentally alien to animation. Merleau-Ponty's theme is the kinesthetic body that moves through a world that is its own, a world that is in some uncanny way itself flesh.

> I too had been struck from the float forever held in solution,
> I too had receiv'd identity by my body,
> That I was I knew was of my body, and what I should be I knew I should be of my body.
> — Walt Whitman, "Crossing Brooklyn Ferry," lines 63-66

I would like to turn to two chapters of Merleau-Ponty's *Phenomenology of Perception* (1945), those entitled "The Spatiality of One's Own Body, and Motility" and "Space." I will then make brief mention of chapter 4 of *The Visible and the Invisible* (published posthumously in 1964), entitled "The Intertwining—The Chiasm."[4]

Merleau-Ponty advances along the *via negativa* of a pathology of the human body. He does so, not to deduce the normal from the abnormal, but to show that the geometric space of modern science, metaphysics, and mathematics is fundamentally pathological. Herr Schneider (Gelb and Goldstein's premier patient, who suffers from severe lesions in the frontal occipital lobe) proves to be the first perfect Cartesian: when he is ordered to perform an "abstract movement"—for example, to raise his arm—Schneider oscillates his head from side to side in order to locate by reflection the direction of "height." Only as a Cartesian "thing that thinks" can Schneider steer his body. In other words, Schneider's own body, his damaged body, is given to him as a problem of Cartesian-Husserlian geometry or of Hegelian mechanics. Correspondingly, one might say that the entire modern conception of space, the sole space that is placed at the disposal of our architects and physicians even today, is uncannily Schneideresque.

By contrast, Merleau-Ponty seeks an understanding of the "style" of Schneider's motor disturbances, as well as of his visual and categorial-intellectual aphasias, in terms of the "intentional arc" that unites this particular subject to his peculiar world. In Schneider that arc has rigidified and lost its elasticity. Even Schneider's sexual morality is rigid and unrelenting, so much so that Schneider may be the first perfect Pythagorean and Puritan as well: women interest him only as "personalities," for, insofar as they occupy female bodies, he says, they are "all the same." Timaeus and Descartes alike would be proud of Schneider—the immaculately moral male, the first truly liberated human being, the first to inhabit, without residue or remainder from the passions of the soul, the world of pure science and pristine cognition.

However, Merleau-Ponty resists not only the "objective," sterilized, and homogenized space of technology and the natural sciences but also the idealized space of the intellectualist tradition, the tradition brought to its apotheosis by Hegel. For idealism is the mere

obverse of the empirical scientific coin, and thus is of a piece with
it. To philosophies of reflection and cogitative subjectivity ("I think,
therefore, I am—at least as long as I keep thinking of thinking")
Merleau-Ponty opposes an incarnate—better, an embodied—philosophy:

> Thus there is another subject beneath me, for whom a world exists prior to
> my being there; a subject that has demarcated my place in the world. This
> captive or natural spirit is my body—not the ephemeral body *[le corps
> momentané]* that serves as the instrument of my personal choices and is fix-
> ated on this or that particular world, but the system of anonymous "func-
> tions" that embrace every particular fixation within a general projection. . . .
> Space and perception in general mark at the heart of the subject the fact of
> its birth, the perpetual companionship of its corporeality, a communication
> with the world that is older than thought. And that is why space and per-
> ception swallow consciousness and are opaque to reflection. (*P,* 294)

That space and perception are birthmarks of subjectivity, and
that subjectivity is neither machine nor ghost but flesh—these are the
principal lessons of Merleau-Ponty's thesis in *The Visible and the
Invisible.* That thesis envisages the "intertwining" of the body and the
world as flesh. In the *Phenomenology,* Merleau-Ponty had written:
"One's own body is in the world as the heart is in the organism: it
maintains continually in life the spectacle of the visible, animating
and nourishing it from the inside; it forms a system with the visible"
(*P,* 235). However, if the human body is *in* the world as the heart is
in the organism, we still have to confront the paradox that there is
an *inside* to the human body that persists in being *out there* in the
world, ecstatically insistent, unless the world as flesh may also be
said to have an *inside.* Here the usual senses of inside and outside
are abashed. We have to contemplate something like *the flesh of the
world* and a space that is the world's *interstitial tissue.* We inhabit the
world and all things in the world in a bodily way: "Thing and world

are given to me with the parts of my body, not by a 'natural geometry' but in a living connection that is comparable—or, rather, identical—to that which exists among the parts of my very body" (*P,* 237). The hand that touches is also touched and seen, both by others and also—though only incompletely—by me.

    The Visible and the Invisible continues to develop this thought of the finitely reversible flesh of the world. Palpation and visibility consist of crossings and recrossings of the leaves of the world. "The thickness of the body, far from rivaling that of the world, is on the contrary the sole means I have of going to the heart of things, making me world, making them flesh" (*V,* 178). The flesh of the world is therefore something beyond a metaphor. It is an *element,* which also means an element *of language,* a στοιχεῖον in the sense developed by the early Greek thinkers up to and including Aristotle. Further, such flesh is an element of *being,* not merely of *becoming,* occupying both sides of Timaeus's bootless division. If "my" body seems foreign to "me," if my being seems to require sloughing off my body, molting this corporeal integument, that is only because "I" am the legatee of an ascetic tradition that has never been at home in our uncanny world and in this uncanny flesh. "I" am the inheritor of a tradition that has preferred the purity of what is already dead to the confusions of the still living.

Thus, moving through the mucous, traversing body and flesh, one does not envisage the skin as the limit of the enveloping body. The limit of the enveloping body could be the corporeal identity of woman, reborn or touched again by its internal communion, and not destroyed by nostalgia for a regression *in utero.* The dissociation of desire and love would in this case no longer make any sense, nor would the sexual be characterized as amoral or nonethical. On the contrary, the sexual *act* would be that by which the other once again gives me form, birth, incarnation. Rather than instigating the body's demise, the other participates in its renascence. In this sense, no other act is its equivalent. The most divine act. The man causes the woman once again to sense her body as place. Not only her sex and her matrix but her body. He situates the matrix in her body and in a macrocosm, removing it from its

possible adherence to   I cannot pursue here in any detail Merleau-
the cosmic by participa-   Ponty's path from the universal flesh of visibility
tion in a microsociety.
(Irigaray, *E*, 55)   to what he calls *intercorporeity*, the flesh of oth-

ers, language, communication, and thought in a
shared world or microsociety. Perhaps one extended quotation will
suffice. It is a passage that takes us from our first sighting of the other
who sees—the other seer, as it were—all the way to lovemaking; and
it is a passage that gives us the flavor of Merleau-Ponty's extraordinary text, his own inimitable brand of tic-talk:

> As soon as we see other seers, we no longer have before us only the look
> without a pupil, the plate glass without tain that gives us the things with that
> feeble reflection, that phantom of ourselves they evoke by designating a
> place among themselves whence we see them: henceforth, through other
> eyes, we are for ourselves fully visible; that lacuna where our eyes and our
> back lie is filled, filled still by the visible, but a visible of which we are not
> the titulars. . . . But what is proper to the visible is, we said, to be the sur-
> face of an inexhaustible depth: this is what makes it able to be open to
> visions other than our own. In being realized, they therefore bring out the
> limits of our factual vision, they betray the solipsist illusion that consists in
> thinking that every going-beyond is a surpassing accomplished by oneself.
> For the first time, the seeing that I am is really visible for me; for the first time
> I appear to myself completely turned inside out under my own eyes. For the
> first time also, my movements no longer proceed unto the things to be seen,
> to be touched, or unto my own body occupied in seeing and touching them,
> but they address themselves to the body in general and for itself (whether it
> be my own or that of another), because for the first time, through the other
> body, I see that, in its coupling with the flesh of the world, the body con-
> tributes more than it receives, adding to the world that I see the treasure nec-
> essary for what the other body sees. For the first time, the body no longer
> couples itself up with the world, it clasps another body, applying itself to it
> carefully with its whole extension, forming tirelessly with its hands the
> strange statue which in its turn gives everything it receives; the body is lost
> outside of the world and its goals, fascinated by the unique occupation of
> floating in Being with another life, of making itself the outside of its inside
> and the inside of its outside. And henceforth movement, touch, vision, apply-
> ing themselves to the other and to themselves, return toward their source
> and, in the patient and silent labor of desire, begin the paradox of expres-
> sion. (*V*, 188-89; English translation, 143-44)

The "strange statue" of lovers' bodies wrapped about one another and rapt to one another, "fascinated by the unique occupation of floating in Being with another life," is in fact the commencement of expression and speech. All talk traces its lineage back to tic-talk. It is as though the Demiurge cannot possibly persuade Necessity until the two of them are wholly absorbed in one another, enmeshed in an economy that loses track of the giving and taking. Following this train of thought would prevent our falling prey to a suspicion that often surfaces in the literature on Merleau-Ponty—the suspicion that his notions of the lived body and the flesh retain too much of the visualist, cognitive, manipulative, instrumentalist, and technicist orientation toward the eye, mind, and hand. However much Merleau-Ponty seems to focus on demiurgic labor and craftsmanship, work and tool, ἔργον and ὄργανον, the tendency of his thought is to promulgate a different sort of organics based on ὀργάω, "I desire," and ὀρέγω, "I swell with lust." Such stretchings and swellings, however, transport us in the direction of yet another remarkably different body space, both ecstatic and unhomelike at once.

Georges Bataille and the Rectification of Man

Bataille's mythopoeic anthropology is both orgasmic and profoundly tragic.[5] His obsession transcends his most beloved fetishes, those of phallus, anus, and enucleated eye: his obsession is the thought that something "miserably miscarried at the beginning of the constitution of the human body" (*VE,* 260). His discourse is thus profoundly linked to that of Timaeus, who, as we have seen, devotes much of his "entertainment" of the goddess (and Socrates) to the pathological and the pejorative: Timaeus offers detailed accounts of illnesses that plague the body, concluding with the illness of sexual irritability, an irritability in *both* sexes that, we recall, woman *alone* miraculously introduces into the universe. Nevertheless, Bataille's account, while linked to that of Timaeus, wrenches the human body into a space that is quite remote from the Pythagorean astronomer's. That remote space is one in which we may find ourselves not so much *against architecture* as *for archeticture.*[6]

The cardinal phylogenetic fact in the development of the human species, in Bataille's view, is its *vestigial unpaired eye.* For there is a third eye, or the trace of a third eye, that is present in all vertebrates. In a number of now extinct amphibians it was indeed a full-fledged, operative, dorsal eye, located at the top of the skull between the two lateral eyes and opening onto the sky. That vestigial eye is the *pineal gland* in us. (Shades of Descartes—who regards the glandular pineal eye as seat of the soul. Bataille would have been delighted by recent research into this endocrine gland that thinks it sees: the pineal body is photosensitive, significant for our sense of the passage of time, and influential as an inhibitor of gonadal activity in males; what it does in females with regard to this third of its functions, and who or what introduced it into their universe, remain mysteries.) Both

> Once during my misspent days in London, while visiting a friend in a clinic, I saw a rubber stamp on the admissions desk with the words "Psychosexual Problem." The attendant turned around and like a fool I did not pick it up and stamp my forehead with it. This is one of the moments of glory that I regret not taking advantage of in my life. It would have hit the third eye. (Ben Nicholson, personal communication, 1995)

sense organ and gland, both harbinger of light and remnant of inner darkness, the pineal eye is for Bataille the birthmark of human futility and fatality. It is the fleshy symbol of a hapless, hopeless struggle against animality and the earth, of a vain attempt to reach the heights of the open sky.

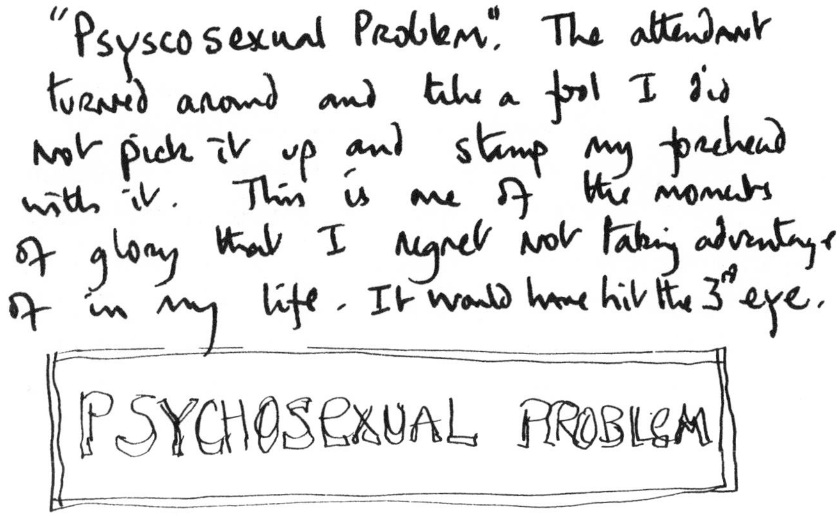

"Psyscosexual Problem". The attendant turned around and like a fool I did not pick it up and stamp my forehead with it. This is one of the moments of glory that I regret not taking advantage of in my life. It would have hit the 3ʳᵈ eye.

PSYCHOSEXUAL PROBLEM

Fig. 26 Ben Nicolson
"Psychosexual Problem," 1995

Presumably, Descartes did not know about the ocular prehistory of *la petite glande* when he chose it as the *siège de l'âme*. However much he remained a devotee of the visualist tradition in philosophy, for which the eye is the window to the soul, Descartes never suspected that the pineal was a metaphor that took itself too literally. The only unbifurcated body he could identify in an otherwise consistently bicameral brain, the pineal body was profoundly *interior* in the brain and yet occupied the most *elevated* position in man, very near the crown of the head, which itself was once a socket (again, the Italian *coppo*). Descartes therefore found himself caught up in the *ascensional trajectory* that the ancients saw described in the very vertical posture of the human body, standing on the earth but "looking up" to the stars. That trajectory, older than Plato's *Timaeus* yet pervasive throughout it, embraces antiquity, the medieval world, and modernity alike: Plato, Augustine, Thomas Aquinas, Freud, and Bataille are all carried in its sweep.[7]

For example, when Aquinas asks whether the human body is fittingly and conveniently disposed, it is man's erect posture that he has in mind.[8] Admittedly, animals on all fours sense more powerfully and move more adroitly than man does. In addition, they have shells, carapaces, fur, and other protective coverings—natural arms of all sorts to shield them. Nevertheless, man's election stands or falls with his erection, which, however, poses some puzzles of its own—among them this one: Man "is more distant from plants than he is from brute animals; yet plants have an erect stature, while the brutes have a prone posture; therefore, it seems that human beings should not have erect posture." Scripture is nonetheless

Angels perceive the foliage of trees as roots drinking from heaven, while the roots of the great tree are seen to be the silent summits. (Alberto Pérez-Gómez, *Polyphilo*, 1992)

adamant: *Deus fecit hominem rectum*. Aquinas replies that man's proper and proximate end (which is "the rational soul and its operations") calls for such erection. As though anticipating modern paleoanthropological and neurophysiological findings, which indicate that those portions of the brain that were once occupied by the sense of smell are now, in *homo sapiens sapiens,* occupied by operations of the "higher intelligence," Aquinas replies that although man has the worst sense of smell he has the best brain: our *pessimum olfactum* is offset by our *maximum cerebrum*. Furthermore, as Timaeus himself had argued, the brain's coolness tempers the heat of the heart by dint of man's vertical posture: a cool head is literally (that is, physically) superior to a fiery solar plexis—and heads and shoulders above a rebellious belly. While man has no horns, talons, feathers, or scales for protection, Cool Head Man "has reason and the hand," the latter being, as Aristotle had called it, "the tool of tools." Finally, Aquinas adduces four reasons for the fitting disposition of *homo erectus* as *sapiens sapiens,* doubly wise:

1. The senses are not for defense alone, but for knowledge and delectation: only man experiences the beauty of food and sex, his head being liberated from the prone posture by which animals grub for food and sniff out partners; man's face, on a head that swivels freely on its base, not only from side to side on the horizontal axis but also up and down on the vertical, is free to know and enjoy things both terrestrial and celestial—even without a pineal eye.

2. The brain in man is not down low in his body, but is elevated above all the parts of his body: *super omnes partes corporis elevatum.* If man's fermenting feet

Aerie. A point high above the house, much like the vantage point when flying in an airplane over the city. The opportunity to put everything in perspective. It has room for more than one person. (Ben Nicholson, "Program Notes for the Loaf House," 1992)

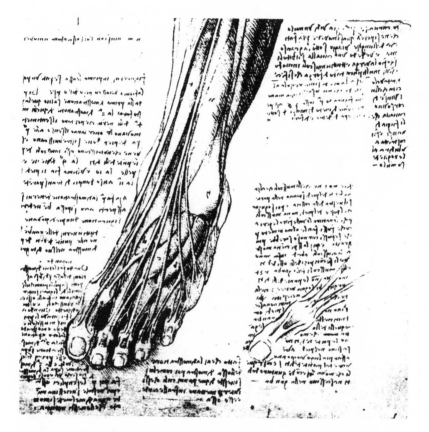

Fig. 27 Leonardo da Vinci (1452–1519)
Myology of the lower extremity (detail), ca. 1510
"All the sinews on the front of the leg serve the tips of the digits of the feet as is shown in the great toe."

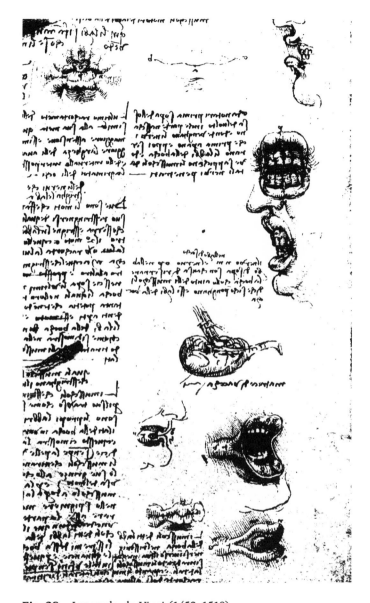

Fig. 28   Leonardo da Vinci (1452–1519)
The alimentary system: lips and mouth (detail), ca. 1504–06
The lips are pursed, pressed, stretched, retracted, and constricted,
exposing their relation to the teeth and to the (sphincter) muscles
of the mouth. At center: the uterus and vagina of a pregnant cow.

smack of earth and underworld, sex and corruption, his head hovers in the aerie of heaven.

3. If man were to scurry about on all four, his hands would soon become pedestrian, and the proper use of his hands, the *utilitas manuum,* would be lost.

4. If man's hands regressed to the status of feet, he would have to seize his food with his mouth; his head would then be oblong in shape, like a pig's or a dog's, his snout extended for convenient foraging; his lips and tongue would be gross and coarse, "lest they be wounded by the world outside." And all this in turn would impede speech, which is "the proper work of reason."

Thus both Aquinas and Bataille anticipate in a startling way the two long notes on human rectification in Freud's *Civilization and Its Discontents* (1930).[9] Retrogression of the olfactory sense, Freud speculates, is a consequence of man's "turning away from the earth." Further, man's erection also makes the genitals visible, inviting both perpetual visual excitation, which is no longer bound to the olfactory periodicity of the menstrual cycle, and shame. "The rectification of man," Freud concludes, "would thus stand at the outset of the fateful and fatal *[verhängnisvoll]* process of civilization."

Freud's immediate purpose is to explain how the *periodicity* of the reproductive process, on the one hand, and the *permanence* of sexual attraction and excitation, on the other, are achieved. The erection of the human posture explains it all. The most important consequence, in his view, is that visual or facial stimulation (the German word *Gesicht* here does double duty, for it means both "face" and "vision") assumes preeminence over the olfactory sense. The effect of visual stimulation is continuous, so that, even when the limbs of the Demiurge and Necessity unravel, these titans remain spellbound by one another. Freud speculates—and it is only a "theoretical speculation"—that the taboo on menstruation arises from such "organic repression," precisely in the way that the gods of an earlier epoch become the demons of the new, their recurrence being henceforth essentially uncanny.[10] The same uncanniness infects the entire evolutionary and civilizing process: humanity's striving after hygiene, the compulsion to get rid of excrement, the repression of anal eroticism, and eventually the quashing of all eroticism in the child. It is "sexuality as a whole" that comes under the ban instigated by the fateful erection of man. As Pope Innocent III, cited in the second treatise of Nietzsche's *On the Genealogy of Morals,* says: the entire physical career of humanity is poisoned by the miasma of sexuality—"impure procreation, nauseating nourishment in the womb, baseness of the materiality out of which the human being develops, horrid stench, secretion of spit, urine, and vomit."[11]

Again the same sin, now clearly unoriginal? (Alberto Pérez-Gómez, *Polyphilo,* 1992)

We seem to glide effortlessly from the doctrines of Timaeus, Thomas, and Innocent, through Freud, up and back to Bataille. However, effort is required. For Bataille's philosophy of nature is as complex as Hegel's, albeit gutted of the latter's categories and placed foursquare not on its head but its buttocks. In Bataille's "Pineal Eye," a savage excess prevails, "delirium escapes from necessity," and science capitulates to "a phantomlike and adventurous description of the universe":

> The eye, at the summit of the skull, opening onto the incandescent sun in order to contemplate it in sinister solitude, is not a product of the understanding; it is instead an immediate existence; it opens and blinds itself like a conflagration, or like a fever that eats the being, or, more exactly, the head. And thus it plays the role of a fire in a house; the head, instead of locking up life as money is locked in a safe, spends it without counting. (*VE,* 82)

The pineal eye, as both sense organ and gland, marks the inter-

section of the two axes of terrestrial life: the vertical axis, extending
the line of the Earth's radius from center to periphery, and the horizontal, tangent to it at any given point on the Earth's surface.
However, the erupting, secreting, ejaculating, and ultimately self-
enucleating pineal eye *reverses* the ascensional trajectory of the vertical axis and *cancels* the centripetal force that organizes the rectification of species-man. If, when man rose to his feet, his anus was
drawn upward into the globes of the buttocks, while the vestigial
pineal eye was drawn downward, ever deeper into the globes of the
bicameral brain, the pineal eruption changes all that, exploding in
both directions at once. If the two foci of the human ellipse are
pineal eye and anus, each having been drawn inward early on in
the course of human development, they revert to the selfsame solitude, which Bataille calls *sinister*—one of the words, according to
Freud's dictionaries, that translate the uncanny. Bataille's unhomelike body threatens to flatten out after a final apocalyptic explosion,
leaving us with the sense that tic-talk will be drowned out by an
uncanny laughter.

Bataille reiterates Aquinas's thesis when he observes that veg-
etation burgeons on the vertical axis (Deleuze and Guattari's rhi-
zomes to the contrary notwithstanding), while brute animal life
extends along the horizontal axis, from snout and eye to tail and
anus (*VE*, 83). To be sure, animals raise themselves from the surface
of the earth "when they exit sleep or when they love"; nevertheless,
they never attain, and do not seem even to desire, complete verti-
cality. "Only human beings, tearing themselves away from peaceful
animal horizontality at the cost of the ignoble and painful efforts
that can be seen in the faces of the great apes, have succeeded in
appropriating vegetal erection and in letting themselves be polarized, in a certain sense, by the sky" (ibid.). What plants do—glori-

ously, according to Goethe's *Metamorphose der Pflanzen,* vainly according to Hegel's *Encyclopedia*—human beings, or "the totality of laughing or lacerated men," do lubriciously and obscenely. Human vision, fixed primarily along the horizontal axis during our day-to-day activities, fetters us to earth and the earthly. The vestigial pineal eye, on the contrary, dreams atavistically of shattering the skull in order to gaze on a sky "as beautiful as death." A sprouting ocular tree, the pineal eye is at once Plato's glassy window of the soul, Descartes's soft and supple gland, and a tumescent penis "drunk with the sun." The pineal eye—whose pineal quality (from *pinus,* referring to its pine-cone shape) is now the acorn or *glans* of a penis—is no longer a tree but a volcano ejaculating lava, sperm, and blood, and also an anus excreting offal (*VE,* 84). The sun toward which the pineal eye strives is a solar anus, a black disc, itself a severed penis, the celestial hyperbole of emasculation.

For these concatenated or conflated symbols, metaphors, and metonymies, no longer really symbols at all but *blancs* (or, better, *rouges et noirs*), Bataille coins a word of his own: his is the system of the *Jesuve.* The *Jesuve* is not only *Jésus,* which in France is both a savior and a sausage, but also *sève,* the sap of Dionysos (*VE,* 259); the *Jesuve* is both the volcano, *Vésuve,* and the goddess, *Vénus;* it is the *je suis* of Descartes, re-marked as the "I follow" (from *suivre*), recently elaborated by Derrida's logic of obsequy.[12] The *Jesuve* is both *dessous* and *dessus,* both the above and the below of the vertical axis; it is the *je subis,* "I submit," of the French, and the *yo subo,* "I ascend," of the Spanish. And so on, into a delirious infinite.

However, the ascent is of a volcano, and toward a lover's grave: the Empedocles Complex. The scene is of ordure rather than verdure. The inverted and interred gibbon, its buttocks alone exposed to the sky and to the affectionate fondling of "a splendid

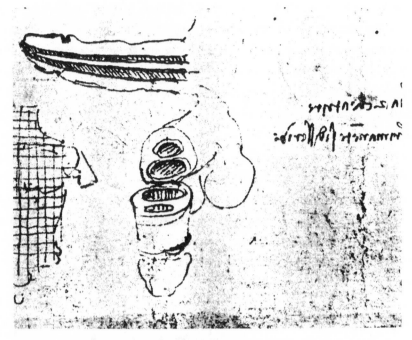

Fig. 29 Leonardo da Vinci (1452–1519)
Genito-urinary system (detail), ca. 1500

Leonardo accepts the view of Avicenna, Galen, Hippocrates—and perhaps
Timaeus—that two penile tubes are essential. The lower, wider tube allows
urine and sperm to pass, sperm providing the "material" for the fetus to
ingest. The upper, more narrow tube, the tube of fiction, attached to the
spinal cord, allows passage of the "spiritual," thoracic contents—namely the
nerve or animal spirits—to the fetus. Bataille would add only two details:
first, that the superior, more rarefied tube runs, via the spine, directly to the
self-blinding pineal eye; second, that the true natures of both tubes are
revealed to a mythopoeic anthropology only when the erect organ is severed.

Englishwoman," embodies or enacts in Bataille's fantasy "the nauseating *JESUVE:* the bizarre noise of kisses, prolonged on flesh, clattered across the disgusting noise of entrails" (*VE,* 86). As a vulgar retort to the rigid Cartesian geometer, and as derisive scorn of the Pythagorean astronomer with his proud eye on the heavens, Bataille gestures triumphantly toward "the excremental orifice of the ape." When the ape's inverted eye bursts the integument of the skull and achieves beatific vision, when the long trajectory of erection and rectification in Western man reaches its apogee, "the universe that seemed menaced by human splendor in a pitifully imperative form receives no other response than the unintelligible discharge of a burst of laughter. . ." (*VE,* 87). *Un éclat,* one must say, *derrière.* And the burst of laughter does not leave tic-talk intact, just as the derisory "splendid Englishwoman" is no embodiment of divine Necessity, of a femininity at last winning its place in the sun after the emasculation of the subject. The unintelligible burst explodes the reproductive romance of τίκτειν, or whatever is left of that romance in a highly technical work such as the present one. Bataille's unintelligible burst, exploding on the scene in 1929, is thus a thought for our time—in which, at least in intellectual and academic circles, heterosexuality is defined as oppressive, reactionary, litigious, and lethal, and in which, worldwide, viral infection emerges as the τέλος of a species at long last rectified.

The *petite glande* of Descartes will have attained its genuine historical meaning only with the help of Bataille's "mythical confusion"; that is to say, only by having condemned itself to "a spectral existence" (*VE,* 89). The specter is a nude humanity bereft of both animal innocence and angelic pride. A naked and destitute humanity is stranded on the nakedest possible plain, a plain bestrewn with cold volcanic ash. "Surrounded by a halo of death, a creature who

Fig. 30 Leonardo da Vinci (1452–1519)
The sphincter ani (detail), ca. 1503
"Definition of a sphincter *[riferramento]* by puckering of the skin, that is, the eyes, nares, mouth, vulva, penis, and anus—and the heart, although it is not made of skin." Apparently unsatisfied with this depiction of the anal sphincter, Leonardo writes the word *falso* alongside the main figure (at seven o'clock). The function of the enema-like projectile descending upon the sphincter (at top center) is unclear.

is too pale and too large stands up; a creature who, under a sick sun, is nothing other than the celestial eye it lacks" (*VE*, 90).

Irigaray and the Ethics of Sexual Difference

Irigaray follows Heidegger's lead, asking what it is *in our time* that calls on us to *think*. What grants us room for thought, what is salubrious to our thought, what filters and fibers the blood of our thought? "Sexual difference," she replies, "is probably the matter for thinking in our time" (*E*, 13).[13] The question of sexual difference grows more and more insistent as our troubles become more and more intractable and our chances smaller and smaller—perhaps even in the work of architecture. For, again in response to Heidegger, Irigaray characterizes our time as the epoch that is caught up in *oblivion of the air,* in which we are as unmindful of the element we breathe as we are of the song on our lips.

> The fundamental dereliction of our time could be interpreted as oblivion and contempt of this element [i.e., the air] that is indispensable for life in all its manifestations, from the most vegetal and animal to the most sublime. Our sciences and technologies remind mankind of its carelessness. They impose on it the most formidable question that could ever be posed, the question of a radical polemic: the destruction of the universe and of the chances for human survival, due to the splitting of the atom and the utilization of it for ends that overwhelm all our mortal powers. (*E*, 123)

Yet this dour view of our chances is countered by a utopian strain in Irigaray's thought, as though (again following Heidegger) thought must struggle to rise beyond both grim pessimism and facile optimism. Irigaray asserts, in the teeth of the bleakest prospects, that the thought of sexual difference may constitute "the horizon of worlds that possess a fecundity still to come," the fecundity of "birth and regeneration," not only for "amorous couples" but also for thought, art, poetry, and language. Irigaray envisages nothing less than a new kind of *making*, a new archetictonic, one might say. She calls it "creation of a new *poiëtique*" (*E*, 13).

Such fecundity would find expression not simply, and perhaps not preeminently, in the fetus, not in the production of sons for the paternal divinity and daughters for his minions, but in the enrichment of lovers' lives. The thought of fecundity, "the fecundity of the caress,"[14] certainly would not scorn the mother's unborn, would not spurn all of gestating humanity—not in a time when that very gestation is under threat of contagion and even extinction; yet it would resist the Hegelian "destiny" for womankind (not unrelated to the Freudian "genital destiny") that moves so quickly and so ruthlessly from sister to mother, maiden to matron. Above all, however, Irigaray wants to resist the "equilibrium of the blood" that Hegel so admires in (his version of) the brother-sister relation, the funereal relation of Antigone to her dead brother (*E*, 114). Such equilibrium amounts to the submission by womankind to the destiny that leaves it virtually no role to play in the sociopolitical destiny of spirit, apart from the woman's embrace of the family dead or the violence of her seduction to war (*E*, 121). The fecundity that Irigaray has in mind is not a polemic. It is "nontraditional," and certainly not "familial" in any familiar sense. The very *places* of mother, sister, father, and brother—the very sites and

Poets. Two friends walked up the street the other day and delivered two finches to our two children. To see the two together, standing on the sidewalk holding a cage of finches between them, gives an inkling of what composes the poetic life. It is a priceless way of existence, the poet says things, does things, and molds thoughts freshly and gives us cause to stop the incessant grind of the day. The poet gives out, at no cost, all day long: it is no wonder that those who are not poetic love to be around those who are. When the will moves the patrons' curiosity, they are rewarded and the poet's life is endorsed. Why are we reluctant to welcome wandering minstrels and why do we still prefer to relegate their ways to the cage of culture, the gallery galley? (Ben Nicholson, "Wandering Domesticity," 1993)

situations of woman and man—shift and are radically displaced. As these sites and situations shift, so too does the meaning—and perhaps the very orthography—of architecture.

Fecundity implies "a revolution in thought and in ethics" (*E*, 14). Every relation of the subject to its world is to be reinterpreted. "World" means the cosmos as such, both the micro- and the macrocosm. Even the gender and genre of God, which in the West has been strictly masculine and solidly paternal, will have to change, and so will the very meaning of space, time, and the human body. In the following passage, Irigaray outlines the implications of sexual difference for space and time in their Kantian distribution, discussed above in chapter 2:

> In the beginning was space and the creation of space. For this is what the theogonies say. The gods, God, create—at the outset—*space*. And time is there in order to serve space, as it were. During the first day or days, the gods or God arrange a world by separating the elements. In the aftermath, the world will be peopled and a rhythm inculcated among the world's occupants. God would be time itself, burgeoning, externalizing himself in his actions in space and in places.
>
> Philosophy goes on to assure the genealogy of the gods' or of God's task. Time will become the *interiority* of the subject himself. Space will become his *exteriority*. (This problem is developed by Kant in *The Critique of Pure Reason*.) The subject, master of time, becomes the axis of the world's administration, along with its Beyond in the instant and in eternity, to wit, God. He operates the passage between time and space.
>
> Would all this be inverted in sexual difference? Where the feminine is lived as space, but often with the connotations of the chasm and the night (God being the space for clarity), and the masculine is lived as time. (*E*, 15)

To think sexual difference in the cosmic terms of (feminine?) space and (masculine?) time is to prepare for the revolution, though not yet to achieve it. "A change in epoch requires a mutation in our perception and conception of *space-time*, in the way we *inhabit places* and the *envelopes of identity*" (ibid.). Nothing is more impor-

Transport toward one another and *reduction of the interval* are the movements of desire (even by expansion-retraction). The greater the desire, the more it wills to surmount the interval, all the while retaining it. . . . The interval tends toward zero with skin-contact. It passes beyond zero when there is passage to the mucous. Or transgression in touching through the skin. The problem of desire being to suppress the interval while not suppressing the other. Because desire can devour place, whether it be to regress to the intrauterine mode in the other, or to abolish in various ways the existence of the other. In order for desire to subsist, there must be double place, a double envelope. Or God, as subsistence of the interval, protraction of the interval, to and in infinity. Irreducible. Deploying the universe and its beyond. In this sense, interval would produce place. Thus sexuality perhaps encounters this aporia or this question in which it rivals the question of God. (Irigaray, *E,* 53-54)

tant for such an epoch-making turn, according to Irigaray, than the thought of the *interval.* The interval, which is the site of *desire,* affects all the rest, and it does so through "displacement of the subject or object in their relations of proximity or distancing." Such undistancing, we recall, implies the very *ecstasis* or rapture of time and space *(Ent-fernung, Ent-rückung).* With regard to the interval, the words *passage* and *transport* are two of Irigaray's most commonly used words.

The thought of the interval, the in-between, is also a thought of residues and remainders *(les restes),* reminiscent of Derrida's treatment of this theme in *Glas.* The in-between is thus a thought of *limits,* of enveloping spaces and enveloped places, hence a thought of *envelopes,* as in the "building envelope" so familiar to architects. "If woman, as mother, is traditionally represented as *place* [lieu] for man, the limit signifies that she becomes a *thing* [chose], with possible mutations from one epoch of history to another" *(E,* 17). The maternal-feminine comes to serve preeminently as the envelope, the container and the outermost limit, of things. Since Aristotle, perhaps even since Plato's *Timaeus,* that envelope slips away from—and therefore also menaces—every thought that would seek to master it.

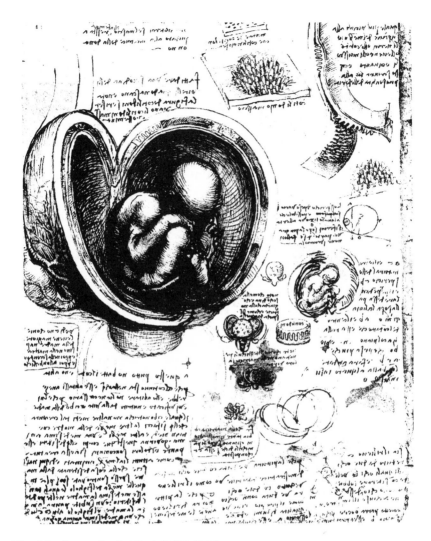

Fig. 31 Leonardo da Vinci (1452–1519)
The fetus in utero, ca. 1510–12

"One and the same soul governs these two bodies [i.e., mother and fetus], and the desires, fears, and pains are felt in common. . . . From this it occurs that the thing desired by the mother is often found impressed upon those members of the infant that the mother herself holds at the time of the desire, and that a sudden fright kills both mother and child." Irigaray fears not the "sudden fright" but the perennial reduction of woman to room—and of room to a site of dominion and mastery. Her thought would preserve the significance of *limits, envelopes,* and *places,* but resist the nostalgia for and the "obscure commemoration" of intrauterine existence.

The maternal-feminine remains the *place that is cut off from "its" place*. She is or becomes without cease the place for the other, who cannot cut himself off from her. She is thus menacing, without knowing it or wanting it, because of what she herself is lacking, to wit, a "proper" place. It would be necessary for her to reenvelop herself, and at least twice—as woman and as mother. Which implies a modification of the entire economy of space-time. (*E,* 18)

There is nothing clear about the process of such reenvelopment, not even for Irigaray herself. Whereas, on the one hand, she celebrates the placental envelope that provides the initial place for every gestating human being, she fears, on the other hand, the intense nostalgia for intrauterine existence, the nostalgia that produces so many regressive effects for women. Fetal envelopment suffers a lifetime of "obscure commemoration," to be sure; the "prenatal sojourn" remains frighteningly powerful in its effects for both sexes. Yet the dignity of that primal place—what Aristotle calls the πρῶτον τόπος—never can or should be gainsaid.

What then is our neighbor? — What do we comprehend of our neighbor, if not his boundaries? I mean that by which a neighbor incises himself or impresses himself on us, as it were. We comprehend no more about him than the changes in us that he causes—our knowledge of him is like a hollow, molded space [einem hohlen geformten Raume]. We attribute sensations to him that his actions call forth in us, thus giving him a false, inverted positivity. We shape him according to our knowledge of ourselves, make him a satellite of our own system: and when he shines or clouds over before us, and even if we are the final cause of both, we still believe the very opposite! A world of phantoms is what we inhabit! An inverted, topsy-turvy, vacuous, and yet complete and upright dreamworld! (Nietzsche, *Daybreak,* no. 118; *KSA,* 3: 111)

One recipient of such criticisms is none other than Merleau-Ponty, whom Irigaray accuses of nostalgia for the intrauterine. We therefore might pause a moment in order to consider her reading of *The Visible and the Invisible.*[15]

Irigaray fears what she calls the "labyrinthine solipsism" of Merleau-Ponty's notion of the flesh of the world. However, the allusion to Ariadne, via the figure of the labyrinth, indicates the double edge of her fear. To be sure, one must worry about the erect, visualist, functionalist aspects of many of Merleau-Ponty's analyses. They often seem to subordinate touch to vision and to prefer the touched-touching self to the touch by and of the other. There is something unmistakably "amniotic" and "placental" about Merleau-Ponty's descriptions of the reversibility of the two leaves of the world as flesh. Yet should one worry overmuch about the "amniotic" and the "placental" if indeed the subject is in the world the way the heart is in the organism? Would not such worry repeat the classic complaint of the activist-mentalist consciousness that feels itself being swallowed up by the anonymous life of the body? Irigaray finds such intrauterine confinement stifling: she wants to be born, to be unbound, to break free; she insists that there be an unbinding and a maturing, that one not mourn forever the intrauterine intimacy with the (m)other, an intimacy that in any case can never be regained. Yet what Irigaray requires of Merleau-Ponty she must also demand of herself. She must allow her many elegiac invocations of the maternal-feminine, of the envelope, of containment, and even of the self-embracing lips of woman to be haunted by her own stifling fears, fears of nostalgia, regression, and "homesickness for the origin," as Freud calls it in "The Uncanny." Merely possessing the genitalia of vulva, vagina, and womb provides no guarantee against such nostalgia. Indeed, such possession doubtless entails dangers of its own, principally the danger that one might unconsciously buy into the doctrine of genital destiny by proclaiming a special privilege for one's insights, which are

> Yet even if we say *khôra* and not *the khôra*, we are still making of it a name. A proper noun to be sure, but a word just like any other common noun, a word distinct from the thing or the concept. However, the proper noun seems, as always, to be attributed to a person, in this case a woman. Perhaps a woman, most likely a woman. Does that not aggravate the risks of anthropomorphism, against which we wanted to be on guard? (Derrida, *K*, 32)

insights reserved for the "other," which one now claims to *be*—
without interval. *(L'autre? C'est moi!)* Passport feminism.

Irigaray is surely right to interrogate the "archaic carnal
ambiance" of Merleau-Ponty's thought of the world as flesh (*E*, 150),
an ambiance that often appears to regress to "a sort of animism, in
which the visible becomes another living thing" (*E*, 161). She is surely right to worry whether the chiasmatic intertwining expresses anything more than primary narcissism, "a prenatal incestuous situation
with regard to the whole" (*E*, 162). Yet how close the affirmation of
this situation comes to the celebration of woman as intimacy of
place—the feast that Irigaray herself is trying to prepare. When her
reading abandons "admiration," loses patience, grows fearful of an
other who may be uncannily feminine in his very masculinity, and
when that impatient reading shortchanges its object, one senses the
painful ricochet effect:

> We doubtless find there a certain elaboration of the carnal. But always in its
> solipsistic relations with the maternal. There is *no trace of the carnal idea of
> the woman-other* [l'autre femme], *nor of the sublimation of flesh with the
> other.* Barely an alchemy of substitution, of placental nourishment. A sort of
> *milles-feuilles,* representing an archeology of the subject, of the world, and
> of their exchanges. But this archeology already existed. . . . (*E*, 168)

What makes the ricochet effect even more painful is the hap-
penstance that Irigaray's highly selective analysis of Merleau-
Ponty's text skips over twenty-two pages, including those pages on
intercorporeity and *desire* that we cited earlier in the present
chapter (*E*, 156-57). There Merleau-Ponty's thought does seem to
approach an other, perhaps even a woman-other. There Merleau-
Ponty is himself attentive to "visions other than our own," which
"betray the solipsist illusion." No reading is innocent, to be sure,
and selection is as inevitable for me here as it was for Irigaray. Yet

it does seem strange that she should pass over in silence that very interval of Merleau-Ponty's text in which the "strange statue" is invoked, that "clasping of another body," embracing "carefully with its whole extension," "floating in Being with another life." No doubt, Irigaray could fix on the word *floating,* so that even here, and perhaps especially here, the amniotic relation would pervade Merleau-Ponty's thought. True. Yet how far removed is the amniotic from the mucous, the fish from the amphibian? Such is the "paradox of expression," which is "elaborated in the patient and silent labor of desire," that Irigaray seems to ignore Merleau-Ponty's *passage* over the archetictonic threshold, the passage that Irigaray herself everywhere else hails and welcomes.

The self-touching of mucous tissue is no doubt different from palpation of the world by the fingertips. Such tissue is no doubt much more alien to "my mastery" (*E,* 159), and it is the ultimate defeat of mastery that Irigaray wants to acknowledge above all else. The ethics of sexual difference, even as it passes by angels on its way to God, remains as mindful of its own limits as it does of the feast. There is as much mourning in Irigaray's thought as there is in Bataille's, though considerably less violence. The interval in-between never entirely disappears in the conflated, the coterminous, or the coextensive; neither sex ever fully knows the other, whatever its passport, however many its entry visas. There is always remainder, residue, and remnant (*E,* 20).

What, then, in order to conclude, are the prospects for a new ethics of sexual difference? Whereas certain oriental cultures have experienced the "energetic, aesthetic, and religious fecundity of the sexual act," with the two sexes granting one another "the seed of life and eternity," the fate of sexual difference in the West has been singularly doleful:

Fig. 32 Leonardo da Vinci (1452–1519)
*External genitalia of the female and anterior aspect of the fetus in
utero* (detail), ca. 1510–12
"The woman commonly has a desire quite the opposite of that of
the man . . . ."

As far as our own history is concerned, we must reinterrogate every aspect of it in order to comprehend why sexual difference never had a chance. Neither empirically nor transcendentally. Why it has always lacked its ethics, its aesthetics, its logic, its religion, the micro- and macrocosmic realization of its emergence or of its destiny.

Certainly, the answer will involve the dissociation of body and soul, of sexuality and the spiritual; it will involve default of the passage of spirit *[passage de l'esprit]*, of god, between inside and outside, outside and inside, and of the shared distribution of inside and outside between the sexes in the sexual act. (*E*, 21)

In Western experience these separate realities—art, science, worship—remain huddled in their separate spheres, in isolated and isolating architectures. They never cross the fluid, mucous boundary of the sexual. God burns his bridges to the sensuous, while angels vaguely yearn apart. Meanwhile, the raptures of the pious allow them to sail in dreams across the chasm of the sensual and the erotic to the desiccated bosom that can only be God's.

> Did not discourse on *khôra* ... designate a yawning gap, an abyss or a chasm? Is it not on the basis of this chasm, "within" it, that the cleavage between the sensible and the intelligible, indeed, between body and soul, can take place and take its place? (Derrida, *K*, 44-45)

Nietzsche dreams of a god who could dance and laugh, Irigaray of a god who could touch. "Who imagines the beyond as an infinite felicity of touch?" No one, not ever. "Never a God who envelops me, wraps me round, cradles me. . . . Loves me carnally, erotically. Why not?" (*E*, 153).

> The "liqueur" decanted by the man in the sexual act? Ambrosial elixir, and from the place itself. (Irigaray, *E*, 56)

What might an archeticture elaborate, by design, in a Merleau-Pontian world, on a Bataillean earth, in an Irigarayan universe? Put negatively, and succinctly, its elaborations could never be exertions of mastery and exercises in technical manipulation. Put positively, though still too cryptically, those elaborations would *respond to* uncoerced materials, fascinated by them rather than bent on dominating them. Archeticture in a Merleau-Pontian world, on a Bataillean earth, and in an Irigarayan universe would be either a series of crossings and recrossings of flesh, visibility, and tactility; or inversions of carnality, of delirious eye and feverish caress; or a delicate exchange of places, without the interval of difference ever closing. It would be either a scene in which every idea is musical or painterly, and thus applied to a timbre, thickness, materiality, or opacity from which it would be inseparable; or a scene in which everything is wrenched from its place and distorted by a creature that confuses itself with creepers and clambering plants—erect, murderous, seemingly unstoppable; or a scene in which tenderness becomes possible again, from the fetus in its pliant envelope to the chastised gods who, having surrendered mastery, remain mindful of the mutuality in lovemaking.

For Merleau-Ponty, the chiasm or intertwining of a fleshed subject and the flesh of the world would not be angular, would not be a symmetrical intersection: a certain soft asymmetry would always prevail in the interlacings of the flesh, allowing our retreat into hollows and uncluttered spaces. For Bataille, those hollows would darken with the terror and trauma of a vain flight from the earth; they would occlude with stellar sickness. Hegel somewhere refers to the scattering of stars across the night sky as a kind of leprosy. For Irigaray, the skin would not be marred, not even in passage through the mucous membrane, as long as one sex does not try to usurp the place of the other.

For Merleau-Ponty, the fleshy application of endogenous tissues; for Bataille, the sacrificial denudation of surfaces; for Irigaray, multiple containments, but no boxing-in. For Merleau-Ponty, articulations of space and reticulation of all the objects in space; for Bataille,

The sliding scale that exists between the imagination and the architect's artifact can now stop at the disarticulation of all spaces, the undoing of all stable objects and processes; for Irigaray, an undoing of all the old objects, which remain too much of a kind, and a rearticulation of the whole. For Merleau-Ponty, sedimenting leaves of experience; for Bataille, limbs stripped of their glory; for Irigaray, one fluid seeping into another fluid by the porosity of the membranes between them. And, to bring an endless series of ecstatic possibilities to a close: for Merleau-Ponty, situations and visitations of visibility, palpation, approximation, and patient interrogation; for Bataille, irruptions and versions—inversions,

what it knows best, the body itself. Once or twice the artificer allows himself the privilege to be in the body and to think of and make things that shimmy around this scale. The extenuated route that exists when the imagination passes through the body, collecting on its way some indicators of realness, stops momentarily when it stands in front of architecture. Before architecture the body sheds everything that it initially held onto to give itself credibility. Once the body has left behind the explicit corporeality, it is left with inexplicit beauty, that elusive substance that doors, windows and walls prefer, in their hearts, to be made of. (Ben Nicholson, "Critical Dimensions: Slide Rules for the Body," *New Dimensions* 18)

subversions, reversions, perversions; for Irigaray, porosity, passage (for example, between time and space), communication by membrane and velleity, ecstasy by osmosis, and celebration of irreducible difference at the feast of carnal reciprocity.

The body spaces of Merleau-Ponty, Bataille, and Irigaray certainly are not identical spaces. The existential is not the execrable is not the elixir. Yet these body spaces have this in common, that they are all outside or beside themselves. Ecstatic. And that their ecstasy eludes the usual modes of mastery and control.

No prosaic thought, such as mine, here, can capture the ecstatic images of an archeticture. Perhaps all I can do at the end is return once again to the outset, to the tale of Timaeus, altering it at the last ever so slightly. For there is no perfect single division, no simple

Passage from one place to another remains for her the problem of place as such, but in the mobility of her very makeup. She moves in place as place. In the availability of place. Her question being to trace the limits of it herself, in order to situate herself there and to offer hospitality to the other. In order to be able to envelop, she must have her envelope. Not only her costumes and ornaments of seduction but also her skin. And her skin must envelop a receptacle. (Irigaray, *E*, 42)

split into two. There are always three, or multiples of three, as though three were the first number. Not in order to reinstate the Hegelian negation of negation, but for the sake of a passage beyond the original image—the so-called paradigm—and its afterimage. For the original is merely the image of a duplicitous structure, the metaphysical structure of image-versus-original, and there are many who say that Father Plato himself gave us all the comic sensibility we need in order to be shaken out of the dream of originals once and for all.

Passage occurs in multiples of three, respecting "the third kind," even if our thought habitually remains stuck on twos—the either-or, neither-nor, both-and, yes-no, plus-minus, good-evil, healthy-sick, male-female of all our binary oppositions. Passage is perhaps what Heidegger is trying to think about in the following passage. The context is Nietzsche's notion of the place of the human body in the cosmos, as one chaos applied to another, or as some as yet unknown third, in which the cosmic seeps into the body as the body passes through the cosmic:

Life lives in that it bodies forth. We know by now perhaps a great deal— almost more than we can encompass—about what we call the body, without having seriously thought about what *bodying* is. It is something more than and different from merely "carrying a body around with one"; it is that in which everything that we ascertain in the processes and appearances in the body of a living thing first receives its own process-character. It may be that *bodying* is initially an obscure term, but it names something that is *immediately* and *constantly* experienced in the knowledge of living things, and it must be kept in mind.

As simple and as obscure as what we know as gravitation is, gravity and

Fig. 33 John Hejduk
"Passage"
In *Vladivostok,* 1989

Walls. Many surfaces in the walls. A three-dimensional wall. The two wall surfaces designed from either side, and then brought together as one. The ambiguous surface that pushes back and forth. The wall as a diaphragm between surfaces; it seeps, it explodes one way and implodes another way. The wall is an extrusion of an entire house, a pilasterized house. How close is the proximity of the outer surfaces? A vestibule is a hollow wall, it allows you to go into a building twice. (Ben Nicholson, "Program Notes for the Loaf House," 1992)

the falling of bodies, the bodying of a living being is just as simple and just as obscure, though quite different and correspondingly more essential. The bodying of life is nothing separate by itself, encapsulated in the "physical mass" in which the body can appear to us; the body is seepage and passage at the same time. Through this body flows a stream of life of which we feel but a small and fleeting portion, in accordance with the receptivity of the momentary state of the body. Our body itself is admitted into this stream of life, floating in it, and is carried off and snatched away by this stream or else pushed to the banks. The chaos of our region of sensibility, which we know as the region of the body, is only one section of the great chaos that the "world" itself is.[16]

Merleau-Ponty, Bataille, and Irigaray, rejoining Blake, Nietzsche, Derrida, and Heidegger, are architectural thinkers of body spaces for unhomelike bodies, bodies caught up in the ecstasies of an uncanny existence. For these thinkers, the body cannot be counterposed to spirit, mind, or soul; for them, the body is eminently alive, alert, aleatory. For them, the body is not so much *in* passage as it is *passage itself.* Passage itself is not embarkation for a world beyond this one and only world. Passage is not transcendence. Passage is "at the same time" seepage, *within* the one and the two, *within* the great chaos of the world of space and time and the microchaos of human bodies. *Passage,* incidentally, is the title of a drawing by John Hejduk.[17]

All that is desired by our hearts can always be reduced to the figure of water. (Alberto Pérez-Gómez, *Polyphilo,* 1992)

A MALADY OF CHAINS
Husserl and Derrida on the Origins and Ends of Geometry, with a Note to the Archeticts of the Future

> Finally, my dear Lou, it's the same old profound and heartfelt plea: *Become the one you are!* In this regard it is necessary, first of all, that we emancipate ourselves from our *chains;* but then, in the end, we must also *emancipate* ourselves from this emancipation! Every one of us, each in his or her own way, has to labor over this *malady of chains,* even after we have shattered them.
> — Friedrich Nietzsche to Lou von Salomé, August 1882

In what follows I shall consider Edmund Husserl's account of the origins of geometry—in his 1936 essay of that title—along with Jacques Derrida's 1962 introduction to Husserl's text.[1] I shall read these texts with a view to the seemingly ineluctable interlacing of architecture, philosophy, and geometry throughout the history of all three fields of inquiry. Prodded by the suspicion that philosophy and architecture alike are facing the question as to how life goes on *after geometry,* I shall take up Husserl's and Derrida's texts as though some ancient concatenation, some ancient chain, were being undone in them.[2]

Husserl announces his project in *"Der Ursprung der Geometrie"* as an "inquiry back *[Rückfrage]* toward the original meaning of geometry," an original meaning that he takes to be still decisive for philosophy in the twentieth century—even if these "original beginnings" of geometry have "foundered" in obscurity (*UG,* 365-66). Husserl inquires back, looks back, moves back through centuries of the Western intellectual tradition, returning along a historical line or chain that ostensibly guides him back to the time when geometry "had to emerge *[aufgetreten sein mußte]*" (*UG,* 366). It had to emerge in order to found architectonically "the *one* philosophy" that according to Husserl has dominated Europe from the very beginning. Yet as Husserl moves back toward the origin of geometry it becomes more and more difficult to take the measure of the architectonic origin he means: the geometry of origins proves to be infinitely more complex than the origin of geometry itself, far more complex than a Euclidean geometry could even dream of being.

In what follows I shall proceed in a way that at least on the surface is quite similar to Husserl's procedure, that is, by reading his "Origin of Geometry" from back to front. I will "inquire back" by citing four extended passages from his essay, following an order that is the inverse of Husserl's order. I shall do this because I regard the earliest passage in Husserl's text as the decisive architectonic gesture of the entire essay—decisive and most problematic. (Derrida agrees that there is a decisive gesture in the essay, but, as we shall see, he locates it elsewhere.) These four passages, read in reverse order, revolve about the axes of *continuity, reactivation, sedimentation,* and *recollection as a chain of repetitions.*

1. Husserl is drawn to the question of the origin of geometry because of the *continuity* that geometry seems to grant the philosophical tradition, from its beginnings in Plato and Euclid to its moment of crisis in contemporary Europe. For each advance in geometry is linked to its predecessors in such a way that a chain is

formed, a chain that is both geometrical and historical. Indeed, the continuity that Husserl has in view derives from European historical time as such. Concerning the continuity of history and geometry, the cumulative advance through new acquisitions or accretions of geometry, Husserl writes:

> That all the new acquisitions express an actual geometric truth is a priori certain, if we grant the presupposition that the foundations of the deductive structure *[des deduktiven Baues]* are actually produced in original evidence, objectivized, and thus have become universally accessible acquisitions. There must have been a continuity that was traversable from person to person, from age to age. It is clear that the method of producing the original idealities from the prescientific givens of the cultural milieu prior to the existence of geometry would have to have been written down and fixed in firm propositions *[niedergeschrieben und fixiert sein müßte in festen Sätzen]*. It is clear, further, that the capacity to transpose these propositions out of some vague linguistic understanding into the clarity provided by the reactivation of their evident meaning would have to have been handed down by tradition, and that such tradition would have to have been permanently possible *[beständig tradierbar sein müßte]*. (UG, 375-76)

Already we catch a glimpse of the architectural metaphor that underlies Husserl's entire venture, the *Bau* (building, structure, construction, tunnel, etc.) that philosophy at least since Kant (recall Rudolf Arnheim's remarks in chapter 2, above) has not been able to live without. We also recognize another of the axial words Husserl has already discussed, *reactivation,* and in his account of writing down and fixing we suspect we are seeing something of the *sedimentation* that has also already been discussed. What remains mysterious is the meaning of "original evidence," *ursprüngliche Evidenz,* the transparent givenness of produced and transmitted idealities or propositions—the *originality* of the transparent givenness that presumably will have to be given when we arrive back at the *origin* of geometry, a doubling and redoubling of origin and originality, giving and givenness, that perhaps ought to give us pause. Whatever these transparent givens may be, we can at this point only be certain that they must be handed down from generation to generation, age to age, and person to person. They must, in Husserl's view, form links in a chain that is continuous and unbreakable. *Reactivation* has something to do with the continuity—the linkage—of such a chain.

2. Husserl has already indicated, however, that the *reactivation* in question is not so simple. Even if the whole body of geometry is handed down from person to person, from link to link, no single person masters the whole of the science, at least not each time a geometric problem is taken up.

> Given the ultimately vast growth of a science like geometry, how do matters stand with the claim of reactivation? And what about the capacity to achieve reactivation? If every researcher labors at his or her place on the structure *[an seiner Stelle des Baues]*, how do matters stand with regard to the hours of interruption and sleep? Must the worker, when he or she takes up the task once again, first of all actually run through and reactivate the entire vast chain of founded findings all the way back to the original premises? Obviously, if that were the case, a science such as our modern geometry would not be possible at all. And yet the essence of the results of every stage entails not only that the meaning of its ideational being come later, factually speaking, but also, because meaning is founded upon meaning, that the earlier meaning contribute to the validity of the later one; indeed, in a certain way, that it penetrate the later meaning *[geht in ihn ein]*. Thus no structural component *[Bauglied]* within the intellectual construction *[des geistigen Baues]* is autonomous; no component, therefore, can be immediately reactivated. (*UG*, 373)

Even though there is essential *continuity* in the tradition of geometric propositions and ideas from age to age, the *reactivation* of these ideas is mysterious. It is transparently given in principle, but absolutely occluded in practice. No worker on the construction (again the architectural, architectonic metaphor) has to—or can—

reactivate the entire tradition, or even his or her piece of it, each morning, or after each coffee break. Husserl explicitly calls the tradition of geometric ideas a *chain,* and he emphasizes that the validity of each link interpenetrates the link before and after it. The problem, then, is how a geometer can start at midchain—or midlink.

3. Before we move to the missing link in the chain of Husserl's argument—the link at midchain, where the geometer seems to be able to start back to work without hesitation or embarrassment—we should take up the question of the mode and method of tradition. Husserl defines it as a writing down and fixing of ideas, transposing them from their vague prescientific language into the cut gems of Euclidian geometry—the axioms, principles, and corollaries of logical thinking as such. Here we arrive at the gesture Derrida calls *"un geste décisif"* (I, 83).

> The important function of the written, that is, of documented linguistic expression, is that it makes communications possible without either immediate or mediate personal address: it is, so to speak, communication become virtual. By its means, the socialization of humanity is elevated to a new stage. Written characters, when viewed purely as bodily, can be experienced in a merely sensuous way; they perdure in the possibility of being experienced intersubjectively in common. Yet as linguistic signs, serving as phonemic signs, they also awaken their familiar significations. Awakening is a passivity; the awakened signification is therefore given passively, in a way that is similar to the way in which every other activity that has sunk back into darkness reemerges once it has been awakened by association, at first passively, as a more or less clear remembrance *[Erinnerung].* As in the case of remembrance, so here too what is passively awakened has to be transformed back, so to speak, into the corresponding activity: it is the capability that is originally proper to every human being as a linguistic creature, the capability of reactivation. In accord with this, the writing down effects a transformation of the original mode of being of the sensible image; in the geometric sphere it effects a transformation of the evidence of the geometric image that is coming to expression.[3] The image is sedimented, so to speak *[sedimentiert sich].* But the reader can let it become evident again, can reactivate the evidence. (*UG,* 371-72)

Reactivation is therefore like the reading of a written text. The oral communications of a prescientific age, vague and imprecise, must be written down not only in order to be transmitted but also in order to attain the clarity that will make them worth transmitting. Like fine silt, or the colloidal dispersion in a wine barrel, the meaning-image *(Sinngebild)* will, when it is written down, *sediment.* Sedimented communication will become transparent again, like the purest water or noblest wine, as soon as its sense is reactivated in full evidence. There can be no question but that such *sedimentation* is a decisive gesture for the *continuity* of a tradition, especially the tradition of a geometry in which each link of the chain or point of the line is contiguous with, or even penetrates, the points or links on either side of it, in the past and future. Yet what does the continuity of sedimentation and reactivation presuppose? How are passive awakening and active apprehension related? Husserl compares them—unless it is something more than a mere comparison—to the function of *remembrance,* as though *remembrance* were a *chain of repetitions,* and as though every linkage (including the geometric) were an act of memory.

4. However, what gets repeated and remembered in geometry? How are the oldest axioms of geometry transposed from vague intimations to firm propositions? How do these propositions attain their validity? In what does their status as ideas consist? Even if we know how such ideas are communicated, whether by word of mouth or by written notation, and even if we know how they leap from one mouth or eye to another, so that they can be passed down as self-identical from age to age, how do they leap into the head of that very first geometer? (Husserl will not be concerned about whether his name was Thales, or whether he can be identified at all.) How

was geometry born from that first geometer as Pallas Athena was born from the (aching) head of Zeus, fully formed and mightily armed? Such a birth necessitates that *remembering* occur as a *chain of identical repetitions.*

> Yet how does the intrapsychically constituted image come into its own, how does it come into intersubjective being as an ideal objectivity, which, precisely because it is "geometric," is nothing at all like some psychically real entity, even though, to be sure, it originated psychically? Let us reflect. Original self-existence in the actuality of the first production *[Das originale Selbstdasein in der Aktualität der ersten Erzeugung],* thus in original "evidence," proffers no sort of perdurant acquisition at all, nothing that could have objective existence. Living evidence passes by, to be sure, in such a way that the activity directly passes over into the passivity of our streaming, increasingly pallid consciousness of something that just-now-has-been *[des strömend verblassenden Bewußtseins vom Soeben-Gewesensein].* Ultimately, this "retention" disappears, but the "vanished" passing away and being past has not become nothing for the subject in question; it can be awakened again. To the passivity of something that is at first obscurely awakened, something that may possibly emerge in ever greater clarity, there belongs the possible activity of a recollection *[Wiedererinnerung].* In recollection, we live through the past experience quasi anew and actively. Now, whenever the originally evident production, as a pure fulfillment of its intention, is the renewed production (the recollected), an actual production necessarily enters on the scene in order to accompany the active recollecting, and in this way, in an original "coverage," there comes to be evidence of the identity: what is now originarily realized is the same as what-has-been, what earlier was evident. Cofounded with this is the capability for an arbitrary number of repetitions *[beliebiger Wiederholung]* with evidence of the identity (identity-coverage) of the image in the chain of repetitions *[Wiederholungskette].* (*UG,* 370)

Readers of Husserl will recognize in the above passage all the familiar terms of his account of remembrance or recollection back into the remote sphere—one of his most famous sets of phenomenological descriptions, conducted during the years 1904-10.[4] It will not be possible here to show how problematic those descriptions are, although we may get some sense of the problems as we recount the stages—trying to forge them into the links of a chain—that Husserl elaborates in the above passage:

1. The problem as stated is that geometric ideas, like all other ideas, take shape in the mind of an individual—they are intrapsychic; yet their status as ideas depends on their coming into their own and achieving objective validity. Husserl wants to know about that transformation, believing that here he will uncover the secret origin of geometry.

2. The first productions of the mind, back in some mythic past before geometry, but also in each moment of our own hectic lives, are fleeting; they could never become ideas with objective validity unless they attained some sort of stability—or *continuity*.

3. The living present in the mind flows and fades away—*but it does not flow into nothingness,* does not fade into the great dark.

4. Even when what-has-just-now-been vanishes out of mind and time, it still can be (re)awakened: the mystery of *temporal consciousness,* or what Husserl called *internal time-consciousness,* will uncover the origin of geometry.

That mystery is itself a chain, one that has at least four interconnecting links:

1. The possible *activity* of recollection accompanies the passivity of an at first obscure and approximate (re)awakening.

2. In recollection, we live through what seemed to have vanished, live through it "quasi anew and actively." This leaves only the *quasi* as a problem, only the *quasi* to make us queasy.

3. An "actual production" accompanies what we recollect each time we remember it, and the mind can compare these two productions side by side, like links in a chain, as it were, determining their identity across the lapse of time.

4. Yet comparison side by side is insufficient: the links of the memory chain must be superimposed, they must "cover" one another without a hint of residue or discomfort or excess—something that is very difficult for a chain with interconnecting forged links to do.

The chain of repetitions can guarantee the identity of mental (re)productions only because internal time-consciousness itself is (quasi) a chain. The chain of repetitions is linked in the way that the moments of time and history themselves are linked. Yet the superposition of links in the chain, while absolutely necessary, remains recalcitrant.

Derrida, in his introduction, indicates the terrible undecidability of this linkage of time and mind, history and ideality. For the linkage of the "living present" to any "retention," that is, to the "just-now-having-been," is doubly indeterminate: in it occurs the blink of an eye—the moment or *Augenblick*—that opens up (to) the future, the future of "protentions," which are as essential to Husserl's analysis as the retentions. Yet when the eye opens (to) the future it is vulnerable to all the accidents that can befall both the eye and the "I." The ego may insist on its capacity to repeat an arbitrary number of times the identical memory; yet the identity of these productions hangs upon that notoriously uncertain opening to and of the future. The living present, Derrida notes, cannot dispense with "this originality that is always renewed by an absolute originality," the *two* originalities in the present instance being considerably worse than one (*I*, 46). Eye and mind confront the danger that everything past will be occluded or distorted beyond recognition in the very next instant, which will be the moment or instant through which the identity of ideal objects will bleed, flow, and fade forever. Derrida writes:

Thus the living present possesses the irreducible originality of a maintaining-now [d'un Maintenant], the foundation of a here, only if it retains the past maintaining-now as such and distinguishes itself from it; that is, it must retain the past as a past present of an absolute origin, instead of merely succeeding upon it purely and simply in an objective time. Yet if this retention is not possible without a protention that is its very own form, initially because it retains a maintaining-now that was itself an original project, itself retaining another project, etc.; and further, because the retention is always the essential modification of a maintaining-now that is always held in suspense [toujours en haleine], always tending toward a next maintaining-now. The absolute of the living present is thus only the indefinite maintenance of this double envelopment. (I, 149)

Husserl hopes that the chain of repetitions will link time and mind, idea and idea, axiom and axiom, himself and the architectonic origin of geometry. Yet the galloping anemia and the death that the maintaining-now can never outrun as long as it is held breathless in the living present will also ruin the putative identity of the contents framed by each link of the chain. If time is undecidably both a punctuated line and a seamless continuum, then it is neither a chain nor a sprocketed filmstrip. There is no documentary of memory: the mind cannot rewind the chain or reel time back, in order to "live through" its experiences again. For its experiences are ecstatic, belonging to the ecstatic temporality and spatiality that have been discussed throughout the present book. The more feverishly the phenomenologist insists on the total coverage and perfect identity of his (re)productions, the more he insists on mastery, the more pronounced his malady becomes. For his is a malady of chains.

A Note to the Archeticts of the Future

There are at least eight explicit references to architecture or *Baukunst* in Husserl's "Origin of Geometry."[5] With the exception of the first, which slights "architectures" as so many decorative styles,

each style devoid of ideas and therefore unworthy of being transmitted in the way that geometry is transmitted, all are references to
the geometry of architecture and the architecture of geometry.
Indeed, one could say that architecture is the site where Husserl's
"Origin of Geometry" betrays the geometry of its architectonic origins—its impossible passion for the chain. For, as we shall see, the
chain has to be chained to the place where all construction starts,
namely, to a *foundation*.

In the second half of his essay, Husserl provides something
like a genealogy of geometry (*UG*, 383-84). He suggests that there
are three stages or phases in its development. First, there is the primal situation of prehistorical, prescientific mankind, where there is
no geometry; yet even here we find something like a predisposition
to geometry, inasmuch as things are never mere physical bodies or
condensations of mass, but are always part and parcel of a human
world. Second, there is the protogeometric era, which comes with
the discovery of (smooth) surfaces, (clean) edges, (sharp) corners,
(clear) lines, and (?) points. The adjectives are the essential qualities
of this Husserlian genealogy, which in fact is the inverse of the
Pythagorean genealogy: instead of one point leaping outside itself
to form the line, the line to form a plane, and intersecting planes to
form a solid in space, Husserl envisages the discovery of the
smooth, clean, sharp, and clear. Of course, by the time he gets to
the *point*, no modifiers remain. The punctual point will be—for
Husserl as for all metaphysicians before him—the foundation at the
heart of each link of the chain. Third, there is the age of technology, ushered in by the techniques of measurement. These techniques
correspond to the introduction of the moral outlook, for the sense
of justice is a sense of jointure and order. Only in this final stage,
instructed by "the art of blueprints for structures," do human beings

pass into "the theoretical view of the world and of world knowledge" (*UG*, 384). That view opens humankind to a view of *"aeter-
na veritas"* (*UG*, 385), conducting them to a priori science, morality, and religion—all of which belong to the origin of geometry and
the geometry of origins.

It is only at this point, the point of the foundation on which
geometry should rest, which is the foundation of geometry itself,
that Husserl's inquiry comes full circle and links up with itself: "Only
'in the unveiling of this a priori' can there be an a priori science that
reaches beyond all historical facticities, all historical environments,
peoples, times, and types of humanity. . . . Only on this fundament
can we base the secure capacity to inquire back *[zurückzufragen]*
from the temporally evacuated evidence of a science to its primal
evidences *[Urevidenzen]*" (ibid.). Not even the evacuation of time
can shake Husserl's confidence in the chains of time, time-consciousness, and history, which will carry him back in dreams to the
point from which the entire architectonic of the West can be
(re)constructed. Dreaming of the hardness, smoothness, and reassuring metallic clink of Piranesi's chains, Husserl's essay dissolves in
conceptual fluff: "[O]nly in the unveiling of the concrete historical
time in which we live, in which our universal humanity lives, with
a view to its total universal-essential structure, etc." (*UG*, 381).

What, then, would "After Geometry" mean? One could have
understood the title of the Berlin Architecture Workshop in German
as *Aftergeometrie,* in the way Kant speaks about *Afterdienst* in the
churches of his time. For just as cult and liturgy can be pursued
obsessively for their own sake, anal-compulsively, so too can geometry become obsessive and deleterious for architecture. Indeed,
insofar as the geometry of origins is a malady of chains, geometries
at some point *must* become deleterious for architectures.

Contemporary architecture must struggle against the dictatorship of fundaments, foundations, technologies of measurement, universalities, and idealities. It dare not despise theory, but it certainly must become suspicious of the "theoretical worldview" of which Husserl is so proud. It must pay greater heed to individualities than universalities, as Derrida suggests in a note to his introduction:

> But how are we to determine the ideality of a work that has only one spatiotemporal incorporation, to which its protoindividualization is tied? how are we to make its ideality appear by varying its factical exemplifications, inasmuch as the exemplifications can only imitate a facticity and not express or "indicate" an ideal meaning? in short, what about the ideality of the plastic arts, of architecture? and of music, concerning which the case is even more ambiguous? (*I*, 89 n.)

More positively, it seems to me that architecture today must labor in the studio on variations, inversions, and creative distortions of Husserl's three eras, especially the pregeometric and the protogeometric. It must learn, for example, to dally with rough surfaces, unclean edges, muted corners, hazy lines—and all of it with no *point* at all. If architecture can make do with less continuity, sedimentation, reactivation, and recollection as a chain of repetitions, it may be able to do more with interruption and innovation. It may then become a labor of love, an archticture.

Archticture—spelling it new—would work toward an ecstatic as opposed to a foundationalist sense of space, time, and the human body. Instead of the ideal chain, it would affirm the "enchained ideality" of a "culture enchained by its own equivocations," an ideality and a culture that Derrida finds in James Joyce rather than in Husserl.[6]

In hopes of emancipation, and heading toward closure, we may want to cry, "Archticts of the world unite: you have nothing to lose but your malady of chains!" Yet phase two of Nietzsche's prescribed emancipation gives us pause. Once we have emancipated ourselves from our chains, he says, we must emancipate ourselves from our emancipation. Though we *have to* surrender the reassuring chains of time and mind, history and geometry, truth and eternity, we will never be sure that we *can* surrender philosophy— provided it is a philosophy of "enchained ideality." No, we will not surrender philosophy. Not even for Nietzsche and Joyce, not even for the sake of our own origins, which are geotropisms without origins or geometries.

NOTES

Chapter One. Tic-Talk

1. *BW,* 361. Indra Kagis McEwen confirms my analysis, noting that Heidegger ignores "the primary meaning" of τίκτω, which is "to engender or give birth." See McEwen, *Socrates' Ancestor: An Essay on Architectural Beginnings* (Cambridge: MIT Press, 1993), 146. Yet she does not pose the question of the relation between the technical paradigm that underlies all "making" and the archaic source of both *poiêsis* and *technê* in lovemaking.

2. See D. F. Krell, *Daimon Life: Heidegger and Life-Philosophy* (Bloomington: Indiana University Press, 1992).

3. Francis MacDonald Cornford, "A Ritual Basis for Hesiod's *Theogony,*" in *The Unwritten Philosophy and Other Essays,* ed. W. K. C. Guthrie (Cambridge, U. K.: Cambridge University Press, 1967), 95-116.

4. Mary Shelley, *Frankenstein, or the Modern Prometheus* (Harmondsworth, U. K.: Penguin Books, 1992), 139.

5. Samuel Taylor Coleridge, *Biographia literaria,* chap. 12, in *The Selected Poetry and Prose of Samuel Taylor Coleridge,* ed. Donald A. Stauffer (New York: Random House, 1951), 232.

6. Compare to the account of the Demiurge and Necessity in Plato's *Timaeus* the creation myth of the *Enuma Elish,* involving Marduk's slaying of Tiamat and the creation of earth and sky from her cadaver. On the Babylonian myth, see Edward S. Casey, *Getting Back into Place: Toward a Renewed Understanding of the Place-*

World (Bloomington: Indiana University Press, 1993), 45: "Not unlike Plato's 'mythical' recounting in the *Timaeus* (whose Demiurge is remarkably reminiscent of Marduk), the *Enuma Elish* depicts a progression from inchoate regions to well-formed places. But what Plato designates as 'Space,' 'Necessity,' or 'the Receptacle'—none of which connotes the idea of an organic body—the anonymous author of the *Enuma Elish* specifies as the fallen body of an elemental goddess." As we have seen, however, Ἀνάγκη is but a thinly veiled goddess, as embodied and as elemental as Tiamat. Even though the Demiurge would like to wield compass and hammer on space and stuff, he is called upon for something else, even in that apparently more rarefied Platonic—or Timaean—world. Casey would say that the Demiurge must play Hermes to the receptacle's Hestia. He writes: "Plato's Demiurge, that arch-geometer and hermetic spirit of the ancient Greek world, must first make connection with the chaotic realm of *khôra*. The necessity of this connection—*khôra* is said to be Necessity itself—is most revealing. For choric space is at once hestial (it is said to be the 'seat' of the emerging cosmos) and topological-participational (since it is elemental and pregeometric). This connection suggests that if they are to describe the places in which human beings dwell, the two dichotomies under discussion . . . [i.e., those associated with Hestia and Hermes] must allow for the confluence of their separate terms" (142). That confluence is what tic-talk is about.

7. Maurice Merleau-Ponty, *Le visible et l'invisible* (Paris: Gallimard, 1964), 261-63. I will cite this work in the text as *V,* followed by the page number; it has been translated as *The Visible and the Invisible* by Alphonso Lingis (Evanston, Ill: Northwestern University Press, 1968). I am grateful to Robert Vallier for this reference to *The Visible and the Invisible.*

Chapter Two. Ecstatic Spatiality

1. Martin Heidegger, *Zur Sache des Denkens* (Tübingen: M. Niemeyer, 1969), 24.

2. Martin Heidegger, *Sein und Zeit*, 12th ed. (Tübingen: M. Niemeyer, 1972), 369; hereafter cited in the body of my text as *SZ*, with the page number.

3. See especially Martin Heidegger, *Metaphysische Anfangsgründe der Logik im Ausgang von Leibniz*, vol. 26 of the *Martin Heidegger Gesamtausgabe* (Frankfurt am Main: V. Klostermann, 1978), sec. 10, no. 6. Cited in the text as *MA*, with the page number.

4. Immanuel Kant, *Kritik der reinen Vernunft* (Hamburg: F. Meiner, 1956), A 34. I will refer to Kant's text as *KrV-A* or *KrV-B*, with the page number. (The designation *A* refers to the first edition of 1781, *B* to the second of 1787.) See the English translation by Norman Kemp Smith, *Critique of Pure Reason* (New York: St. Martin's Press, 1965).

5. Augustine, *Confessions*, bk. 10, chap. 17. I have used the Loeb Classical Library edition (Cambridge: Harvard University Press, 1979) throughout.

6. Martin Heidegger, *Kant und das Problem der Metaphysik*, 4th, exp. ed. (Frankfurt am Main: V. Klostermann, 1973), cited in my text as *KPM*, with the page number.

7. Rudolf Arnheim, *The Dynamics of Architectural Form* (Berkeley: University of California Press, 1977), 272-74; hereafter cited as *DAF*, followed by the page number.

8. Human spatiality is not the homogeneous space—the space of Galileo and Newton—that Heidegger perceives to be the space of modern science, metaphysics, and mathematics. In *What Is A Thing?* Heidegger enumerates the following points concerning such space: "1. Newton's axiom begins with *corpus omne*, 'every body.'

That means that the distinction between earthly and celestial bodies has become obsolete. The universe is no longer divided into two well-separated realms, the one beneath the stars, the other the realm of the stars themselves. All natural bodies are essentially of the same kind. The upper realm is not a superior one. 2. In accord with this, the priority of circular motion over motion in a straight line also disappears. And although now, on the contrary, motion in a straight line becomes decisive, still this does not lead to a division of bodies and of different domains according to their kind of motion. 3. Accordingly, the distinguishing of certain places also disappears. Each body can in principle be in any place. The concept of place itself is changed: place no longer is where the body belongs according to its inner nature, but only a position in relation to other positions." *BW,* 286. See also Heidegger's remarks on the modern scientific conception of homogeneous space in "Building Dwelling Thinking," in *BW,* 357-58.

9. Martin Heidegger, *Kunst und Raum* (St. Gallen: Erker Verlag, 1969), 6; cited in the body of my text as *KR,* with the page number.

10. On "ritual," see Spiro Kostof, *A History of Architecture: Settings and Rituals* (New York: Oxford University Press, 1985), 19 A.

11. In turn, on architecture's "inaugural value" for Hegelian aesthetics as a whole, see Denis Hollier, "The Hegelian Edifice," in Hollier, *Against Architecture: The Writings of Georges Bataille,* trans. Betsy Wing (Cambridge: MIT Press, 1989), 3-13.

12. G. W. F. Hegel, *Vorlesungen über die Ästhetik II,* in *Werke in zwanzig Bänden,* Theorie Werkausgabe (Frankfurt am Main: Suhrkamp, 1970), 14: 326; cited in my text as *VA,* followed by either section (§) number or by volume and page.

13. That was the hypothesis I tried to test in a studio session with Don Bates at the University of Florida in November 1989. None of the students' drawings survive, as far as I am aware. For what follows—on Hegel's mechanics of space and time—see Hegel's *Enzyklopädie der philosophischen Wissenschaften im Grundriß (1830), zweiter Teil, Die Naturphilosophie,* in *Werke* (cited in n. 12, above) 9: 41-55, cited in my text as *EpW,* followed by section (§) number or volume and page. For an English translation, see *Hegel's Philosophy of Nature,* trans. M. J. Petry (Atlantic Highlands, NJ: Humanities Press, 1970), 223-36.

14. See Jacques Derrida, *Mémoires d'aveugle: L'Autoportrait et autres ruines* (Paris: Réunion des Musées Nationaux, 1990); translated by Michael Naas and Pascale-Anne Brault as *Memoirs of the Blind* (Chicago: University of Chicago Press, 1993).

15. Schelling cites Baader's 1807 essays, "On the Assertion that No Use of Reason Can Be Evil," and "On the Unmoving and on Flux," in his treatise *On the Essence of Human Freedom,* published in 1809, reprinted in F. W. J. Schelling, *Sämtliche Werke* (Stuttgart: Cotta, 1860), 7: 366 n.

16. On the circle in Aristotle and Hegel, see Jacques Derrida, "Ousia et grammé," in *Marges—de la philosophie* (Paris: Minuit, 1972), esp. 61 and 78. Translated by Alan Bass as *Margins of Philosophy* (Chicago: University of Chicago Press, 1982), 29-67, esp. 53 and 67.

17. *EpW* (cited in n. 13, above), § 258. Aristotle had developed this classic, negative, punctilious account of presence in his "treatise on time," *Physics* 4. 10-14.

18. Maurice Merleau-Ponty, *Phénoménologie de la perception* (Paris: Gallimard, 1945), 484. Translated by Colin Smith as *Phenomenology of Perception* (London: Routledge, 1962). I cite the French edition in my text as *P,* followed by the page number.

19. Martin Heidegger, *Phänomenologische Interpretationen zu Aristoteles: Einführung in die phänomenologische Forschung,* vol. 61 of the *Martin Heidegger Gesamtausgabe* (Frankfurt am Main: V. Klostermann, 1985), 130.

20. *Physics* 4. 13; 222b 14-22. I cite the Oxford Classical Texts edition by W. D. Ross (Oxford: Oxford University Press, 1973) throughout.

21. G. W. F. Hegel, *Über die wissenschaftliche Behandlungs-arten des Naturrechts, etc.* in *Werke* (cited in n. 13, above), 2: 529. See also Derrida's discussion of the significance of this passage in *Glas* (Paris: Galilée, 1974), 123 A; translated by John P. Leavey Jr. and Richard Rand as *Glas* (Lincoln: University of Nebraska Press, 1986), 106-7 A.

22. Martin Heidegger, *Die Grundprobleme der Phänomen-ologie,* vol. 24 of the *Martin Heidegger Gesamtausgabe* (Frankfurt am Main: V. Klostermann, 1975), 377. Henceforth cited as *GP,* followed by the page number.

23. This diagram appears in Martin Heidegger, *Schellings Abhandlung über das Wesen der menschlichen Freiheit (1809),* ed. Hildegard Feick (Tübingen: M. Niemeyer, 1971), 164.

24. Jean Genet, *The Studio of Alberto Giacometti,* in *Œuvres complètes* (Paris: Gallimard, 1979), 5: 39-73; quoted in Derrida, *Glas* (cited in n. 21, above), 93 B/80 B.

25. Jacques Derrida, "Freud and the Scene of Writing," in *Écriture et la différence* (Paris: Seuil, 1967), 293-340; translated by Alan Bass as *Writing and Difference* (Chicago: University of Chicago Press, 1978), 196-231.

Chapter Three. Unhomelike Places

1. These sections of mine could be regarded as responses to Anthony Vidler's wonderful book, *The Architectural Uncanny:*

Essays in the Modern Unhomely (Cambridge: MIT Press, 1992), which I came to know, however, only after my own sections were written. Vidler's argument runs as follows: "Architecture has been intimately linked to the notion of the uncanny since the end of the eighteenth century. At one level, the house has provided a site for endless representations of haunting, doubling, dismembering, and other terrors in literature and art. . . . But beyond this largely theatrical role, architecture reveals the deep structure of the uncanny in a more than analogical way, demonstrating a disquieting slippage between what seems homely and what is definitively unhomely. As articulated theoretically by Freud, the uncanny or *unheimlich* is rooted by etymology and usage in the environment of the domestic, or the *heimlich,* thereby opening up problems of identity around the self, the other, the body and its absence: thence its force in interpreting the relations between the psyche and the dwelling, the body and the house, the individual and the metropolis" (Vidler, ix-x).

2. I shall quote the *Studienausgabe* of Freud's works (Frankfurt am Main: S. Fischer, 1982) throughout, citing it as *StA,* by volume and page. *"Das Unheimliche"* appears at 4: 241-74. For Heidegger's 1925 text, see *Prolegomena zur Geschichte des Zeitbegriffs,* vol. 20 of the *Martin Heidegger Gesamtausgabe* (Frankfurt am Main: V. Klostermann, 1979; translated by Theodore Kisiel as *The History of the Concept of Time: Prolegomena* (Bloomington: Indiana University Press, 1985). In my text I will cite *Gesamtausgabe* vol. 20 as *PGZ,* followed by the page number. On the unhomelike in Heidegger, see now Fabio Ciaramelli, "The Loss of Origin and Heidegger's Question of *Unheimlichkeit,"* *Epoché: A Journal for the History of Philosophy* (Brigham Young University) 2, no. 1 (1994): 13-33.

3. R. M. Rilke, *Werke in zwei Bänden* (Leipzig: Insel, 1953), 2:

39-41; quoted in *GP* (cited in n. 22 of chap. 2), 244-46. My thanks to Will McNeill for the reference to Rilke. The translation is mine.

4. For a discussion of Heidegger and Rilke, see the introduction and chap. 9 of my *Daimon Life: Heidegger and Life-Philosophy* (cited in n. 2 of chap. 1, above).

5. Heidegger, *Phänomenologische Interpretationen zu Aristoteles* (cited in n. 19 of chap. 2), 131-55.

6. See Freud, *Über den Gegensinn der Urworte* (1910), in *StA* (cited in n. 2, above) 4: 227-34.

7. Baurmann was at that time a member of the Laboratory of Primary Studies in Architecture (LoPSiA), directed by Don Bates, at the Cité Radieuse of Le Corbusier in Briey-en-forêt, France.

8. Daniel Libeskind, in John Hejduk, *The Mask of Medusa* (New York: Rizzoli, 1985), 11.

9. See D. Martin Luther, *Die gantze Heilige* [N.B.: not *Heimliche*] *Schrift*, ed. Hans Volz, Heinz Blanke, and Friedrich Kur, 3 vols. (Munich: Deutscher Taschenbuch Verlag, 1974), *Anhang*, 3: 339.

10. Martin Heidegger and Eugen Fink, *Heraklit* (Frankfurt am Main: V. Klostermann, 1970), 234.

11. *StA*, 4: 266. See the thought-provoking reading of *repetition* in Freud's sandman interpretation in Neil Hertz, *The End of the Line: Essays on Psychoanalysis and the Sublime* (New York: Columbia University Press, 1985), 97-121. I have not even ventured to take into account here the vast amount of literature on Freud's reading (see *The End of the Line*, 246-48, which cites Cixous, Deleuze, Derrida, Gasché, Kofman, and Samuel Weber, among others). I am grateful to Cynthia Chase for recommending Hertz to me, and for our discussion.

12. *SZ* (cited in n. 2 of chap. 2), §34, 163; see Derrida's recent *fourth "Geschlecht,"* "Heidegger's Ear: Philopolemology," in *Reading*

Heidegger: Commemorations, ed. John Sallis (Bloomington: Indiana University Press, 1992), 163-218.

13. E. T. A. Hoffmann, *Der Sandmann* (Stuttgart: P. Reclam, 1969), 10; cited throughout as *S,* followed by the page number.

14. Derrida, *Mémoires d'aveugle* (cited in n. 14 of chap. 2, above); see 65-66 n. 59/62-63 n. 59 on Hoffmann's *Der Sandmann.*

15. Jacques Derrida, *De l'esprit: Heidegger et la question* (Paris: Galilée, 1987), 11; translated by Geoffrey Bennington and Rachel Bowlby as *Of Spirit: Heidegger and the Question* (Chicago: University of Chicago Press), 1.

16. See Pierre Klossowski, *Nietzsche et le cercle vicieux* (Paris: Mercure de France, 1969). I have discussed Klossowski in my *Of Memory, Reminiscence, and Writing: On the Verge* (Bloomington: Indiana University Press, 1990), chap. 7, and in my *Infectious Nietzsche* (Bloomington: Indiana University Press, 1996), chap. 11.

17. Martin Heidegger, *Zollikoner Seminare: Protokolle— Gespräche—Briefe,* ed. Medard Boss (Frankfurt am Main: V. Klostermann, 1987).

18. Martin Heidegger, *Beiträge zur Philosophie (Vom Ereignis),* vol. 65 of the *Martin Heidegger Gesamtausgabe* (Frankfurt am Main: V. Klostermann, 1989). For the text by Heinrich Heine, see Heine's *Sämtliche Werke,* ed. Jost Perfahl (Munich: Winkler Verlag), 2: 707-28; see also "Die Göttin Diana," 2: 729-39.

Chapter Four. Unhomelike Bodies

1. Leonardo's hesitation with regard to the designation of first and second causes perhaps has to do with the difference between temporal and ontological priority. In any case, the two causes surely have to do with the difference in detail between the two depicted sexes. Note that the male figure—with face, chevelure, a spine,

and a leg to stand on—is more refined and defined, whereas Necessity is largely reduced to womb and breast. In the male, the meaner ("second") cause of existence is material, spermatic, and alimentary; it passes through the lower and grosser of the two traditionally accepted but fictitious penile ducts. The more elevated ("first") cause, which is spiritual, spinal, and thoracic, passes through the superior duct: note in the male figure the (fictitious) vesicle that connects the spinal cord to the upper penile tube. Note also the (fictitious) vesicle that connects uterus and breast in the female—ostensibly enabling superfluous menses to be transformed into milk during pregnancy. Note finally the (fictitious) direct access of the ejaculated sperm to the uterus itself. Archeticture has no objection to fictions, but seeks greater variety and balance in them, and less will to divide and conquer.

2. See Marsilio Ficino's translation of *Timaeus* 52b 3, λογισμῷ τινι νόθῳ, in *Platonis philosophia etc.* (Zweibrücken: Studiis Societatis Bipontinae, 1786), 9: 249. Cf. Schelling, *Werke,* 7: 174, and Hieronymus Müller's translation in Plato, *Werke* (Hamburg: Rowohlt, 1959), 174. For a more detailed discussion of these paradoxes, see my "Female Parts in *Timaeus,*" *Arion: A Journal of Humanities and the Classics,* n. s., 2 (1975): 400-21; and chap. 1 of my *Of Memory, Reminiscence, and Writing* (cited in n. 16 of chap. 3), esp. 36-39. Finally, readers should note the recent discovery and publication of Schelling's 1794 commentary on *Timaeus,* now vol. 4 of the *Schellingiana,* ed. Hartmut Buchner (Stuttgart: Frommann-Holzboog, 1994); see esp. 74-75, the concluding pages of the manuscript, in which Schelling leaves untranslated the phrase λογισμῷ τινι νόθῳ, but relates it to the Kantian form of outer intuition, discussed in chap. 2, above.

3. On the entire question of the χώρα, see Jacques Derrida,

Khôra (Paris: Galilée, 1993), cited in my text as *K*, with the page number.

4. Merleau-Ponty, *Phénoménologie de la perception* (cited in n. 18 of chap. 2), pt. 1, chap. 3, and pt. 2, chap. 2; and *Le visible et l'invisible* (cited in n. 7 of chap. 1), 172-204. The *Phénoménologie* I will cite in my text as *P*, *Le Visible* as *V*, followed by the page number.

5. I shall restrict myself in what follows to an early text of Bataille, "The Pineal Eye," written circa 1929, about the time Heidegger was teaching his one and only course in theoretical biology. See Georges Bataille, *Œuvres complètes* (Paris: Gallimard, 1970), 2: 21-35; translated in Bataille, *Visions of Excess: Selected Writings, 1927-1939*, ed. Allan Stoekl (Manchester, U. K.: Manchester University Press, 1985), 79-90; cited in my text as *VE*, with page number. See also my "Paradoxes of the Pineal: From Descartes to Georges Bataille," in *Philosophy: Proceedings of the Royal Institute of Philosophy*, ed. A. Phillips Griffiths (Cambridge, U. K.: Cambridge University Press, 1987), 215-28. On Heidegger's biology course, see chap. 3 of Krell, *Daimon Life: Heidegger and Life-Philosophy* (cited in n. 2 of chap. 1).

6. On Bataille and architecture, see Vidler, *The Architectural Uncanny* (cited in n. 1 of chap. 3), 136-45. Vidler emphasizes Bataille's opposition to architectural monumentality and to the alliance of architecture with political oppression, relating Bataille's architecture of resistance to the work of Peter Eisenman. And, above all, see Denis Hollier, "The Caesarean," in *Against Architecture* (cited in n. 11 of chap. 2), 74-170.

7. On ascensional and descensional modes of thinking, see my "Descensional Reflection," the final section of chap. 3 of *Infectious Nietzsche* (cited in n. 16 of chap. 3, above). On the macro- and microcosmic hierarchy of the erect body—head, thoracic cavity, and

gutwall-to-feet—see Leo Steinberg, *The Sexuality of Christ in Renaissance Art and in Modern Oblivion* (New York: Pantheon, 1983), 27-28, 72, and esp. 143-44, which I cite here in part: "The human body as a hierarchical system is a conceit of Late Antiquity, if not older. [As we have seen, it is of course already ancient by late antiquity!]. According to Artemidorus, 'many dream interpreters think that the feet signify menials. . . .' Inevitably, such or similar rank ordering was applied to the Incarnation; head and feet respectively polarized the divine and the human. Thus Eusebius: 'The nature of Christ is twofold; it is like the head of the body in that He is recognized as God, and comparable to the feet in that for our salvation He put on manhood as frail as our own. . . .'" Steinberg refers to Ernst Kantorowicz, *The King's Two Bodies,* and that work's emphasis on the theme of *pedes in terra, caput in coelo,* "feet on earth, head in heaven." Steinberg observes that the boundaries of the hierarchical body often fluctuate, but that the inferior parts cover most of the corporeal territory—that the feet, for example, are a standard biblical euphemism for the genitalia. Steinberg comments: "Within the inferior region, further differentiation would serve no useful symbolic purpose; what matters is the contrast to the superior dignity of head and breast."

    8. *Summa theologiae, Prima pars,* q. 91, a. 3. I use the "Biblioteca de Autores Cristianos" edition (Madrid: La Editorial Catolica, 1961) throughout.

    9. *StA* (cited in n. 2 of chap. 3), 9: 229-30, 235-36. See also letters 55 and 75 to Wilhelm Fließ in Freud, *Anfänge der Psychoanalyse* (New York: Imago, 1950), 198-99 and 246. See also Sandor Ferenczi's astonishing speculative work of 1924, *Versuch einer Genitaltheorie,* in Ferenczi, *Schriften zur Psychoanalyse,* ed. Michael Balint, 2 vols. (Frankfurt am Main: S. Fischer, 1982), 2: 317-

400; translated by Henry Alden Bunker as *Thalassa: A Theory of Genitality* (New York: W. W. Norton, 1968).

10. One must pose some larger speculative questions here. What happens when periodicity is replaced by an effect of permanence, the permanence of presence in the face, a face that excites but also—since it is as exposed to view as the genitals—calls forth shame? See Jacques Derrida, "Spéculer—sur Freud," in his *La carte postale de Socrate à Freud et au-délà* (Paris: Aubier-Flammarion, 1980), 275-437; translated by Alan Bass as *The Post Card* (Chicago: University of Chicago Press, 1987), 257-386.

11. See Friedrich Nietzsche, *Zur Genealogie der Moral: Eine Streitschrift* (Leipzig: C. G. Naumann, 1887), treatise 2, §7, 54. Leo Steinberg cites Pope Innocent III, *On the Misery of the Human Condition*, as follows: "Everyone knows that intercourse, even between married persons, is never performed without the itch of the flesh, the heat of passion, and the stench of lust. Whence the seed conceived is fouled, smirched, corrupted, and the soul infused into it inherits the guilt of sin. . . . " Steinberg, *Sexuality of Christ* (cited in n. 7, above), 46 n. 41.

12. See Jacques Derrida, *Otobiographies* (Paris: Galilée, 1984), esp. 66.

13. That is, Luce Irigaray, *Éthique de la différence sexuelle* (Paris: Minuit, 1984), 13. In the body of my text I cite Irigaray's text as *E*, followed by the page number.

14. See Irigaray's response to Emmanuel Levinas, in *E*, 173-79.

15. Irigaray's reading appears in the penultimate section of *E*, 143-71.

16. Martin Heidegger, *Nietzsche*, 2 vols. (Pfullingen: G. Neske, 1961), 1: 565-66; translated by D. F. Krell et al., as *Nietzsche*, 4 vols. (San Francisco: HarperCollins, 1991), 3: 79-80.

17. John Hejduk, *Vladivostok* (New York: Rizzoli, 1989), 249; see also 229.

Appendix. A Malady of Chains

1. Husserl's "Der Ursprung der Geometrie" is attached as an appendix to Edmund Husserl, *Die Krisis der europäischen Wissenschaften und die transzendentale Phänomenologie,* ed. Walter Biemel, vol. 6 of *Husserliana* (The Hague: M. Nijhoff, 1954), 365-86; Jacques Derrida's "Introduction" appears in Edmund Husserl, *L'Origine de la géométrie,* trans. Jacques Derrida (Paris: Presses Universitaires de France, 1962), 3-171. I shall refer to the first as *UG* and the second as *I,* followed by page numbers, in the body of my text.

2. "After Geometry" was the title chosen by Don Bates and Peter Davidson for the Berlin Architecture Workshop in the summer of 1996.

3. The German sentence is difficult to unravel: "Danach vollzieht sich also durch das Niederschreiben eine Verwandlung des ursprünglichen Seinsmodus des Sinngebildes, in der geometrischen Sphäre der Evidenz des zur Aussprache kommenden geometrischen Gebildes." Derrida has: "Ainsi s'accomplit donc, grâce à la notation écrite, une conversion du mode-d'être originaire de la formation de sens, [par exemple] dans la sphère géométrique, de l'évidence de la formation géométrique venant à énonciation," which we might render as follows: "Thus, thanks to written notation, a conversion of the originary mode-of-being of the formation of meaning is achieved, [for example] in the sphere of geometry, a conversion of the evidence of the geometric formation coming to enunciation" (*I,* 186-87).

4. I have offered a critical account of these analyses in Krell,

"Phenomenology of Memory from Husserl to Merleau-Ponty," *Philosophy and Phenomenological Research* 42, no. 2 (June 1982): 492-505; see also the discussion of the absolute past in Krell, *Of Memory, Reminiscence, and Writing* (cited in n. 16 of chap. 3), 179-87, and elsewhere.

    5. *UG*, 368 (cited in n. 1, above): "oder wie Architekturen und dergleichen Erzeugnisse"; 373: "an seiner Stelle des Baues arbeitet . . . kein Bauglied inmitten des geistigen Baues"; 375: "bei den großen Erkenntnisbauten der Geometrie und der sogenannten 'deduktiven' Wissenschaften"; 375: "die Grundlagen des deduktiven Baues"; 378: "diesen logischen Bau bis ins Letzte in Evidenz verant-worten"; 380: "in Enthüllung der konkreten historischen Zeit, in der wir leben, in der unsere Allmenschheit lebt, hinsichtlich ihrer total-en wesensallgemeinen Struktur"; 384: "Kunst der Aufrisse für Bauten"; 385: "Nur auf diesem Fundament."

    6. See Derrida's extraordinary contrast between Joyce and Husserl in *I* (cited in n. 1, above), 104-5.

INDEX

Note: page numbers in italic type refer to illustrations of or by the listed entry.

rhetoric, 20–21, 26, 50, 58, 102–3; *see
also* affects, Aristotle, letters, literature, speech, word
Rilke, Rainer Maria (1875–1926), 86,
95–97, 195–96n. 3, 4
Rimbaud, Arthur (1854–1891), 99
ritual, 2, 56, 58, 189n. 3, 192n. 10; *see
also* Kostof, myth, sacrifice
room, *der Raum,* 3, 6–7, 15, 28, 32,
54–55, 96, 149, 159, 163; see also
khôra, locale, place, receptacle,
space
Rossi, Aldo, 91
Ruck, start, shock, 78–79, 103; *see also*
detonation, rapture/rupture
ruinance, ruination, ruins, 7, *40, 51,
58, 59, 67, 69, 75,* 76, 86, 91, 95,
97, 102, 109, 138, 184, 193n. 14; *see
also* falling

S

sacrifice, 7, 84, 170; *see also* ritual
Salinger, J. D., 118
Sallis, John, 197n. 12
Salomé, Lou von (Andreas-Salomé,
1861–1937), 175
Sanders, Daniel, 109, 112, 114–15, 121,
124
"The Sandman," 94, 109, 196n. 11,
197n. 13; *see also* Freud, Hoffmann,
uncanny
Sartre, Jean-Paul (1905–1980), 128
scapegoating, 113–14
Schelling, Friedrich Wilhelm Joseph
von (1775–1854), 63, 66, 81, 101,
108, 112, 121, 137, 193n. 15, 194n.
23, 198n. 2
Schlegel, Friedrich (1772–1829), 60
Schopenhauer, Arthur (1788–1860), 97
sciences, the natural, 2, 62, 140–41,
153, 159, 169, 178, 186, 191–92n. 8
sea, *31,* 72, 82; *see also* Ferenczi, liquid, water

secret, *heimlich,* 54, 69, 101, 105, 108,
111–13, 116, 121, 137, 182; *see also*
closets, uncanny, unhomelike
sections, architectural, 7, 86, 89, 91–92,
95, 139, 194–95n. 1
sedimentation, 171, 176–77, 179–80,
187; *see also* geometry, letters, writing
seepage, 24, 171–72, 174; *see also* fluid,
flux, passage, water
seizure. *See* ἔκστασις, rapture/rupture
sense, intelligibility, meaning, 6, 8,
12–13, 16, 20–21, 29, 35, 45, 50, 54,
56–57, 60–62, 65, 74, 93–94, 108,
112, 123, 137, 142, 143, 180, 182,
185, 187, 202n. 3
    inner and outer, in Kant, 45–48,
    50, 53
senses, the five, 22, 34, 45, 55, 63, 78,
123, 136, 146, 148–49, 152–53
sensibility, sensitivity, 45, 65, 94, 172,
174; *see also* responsiveness
sensible, the, 20–23, 65, 136–38, 164,
169, 179; *see also* materials, perception
sensuality, 26, 36, 169, 201n. 11; *see
also jouissance,* lovemaking, sex,
tic-
settling, founding, κτίζω, κτι-, 15–16,
55–56; *see also* building, dwelling,
foundation
sex, 12, 15, 17, 20, 26–27, 33–34, 57,
74, 84, 125, 141, 143, *147,* 149,
152–53, 157, 159–70, 197–98n. 1,
199–200n. 7, 201n. 11, 13; *see also*
caress, desire, erotic, gender, genitalia, lovemaking, reproduction, *tic-*
sexual difference, *69,* 159–69; *see also*
female, feminine, feminist discourses, gender, male, masculine
Shakespeare, William (1564–1616), 29
Shelley, Mary Wollstonecraft (1797–
1851), 24, 115, 189n. 4; see also
Frankenstein